Cooperstown

1998

ALL - STAR CAMP
August 16 – 20, 1998

DOUBLEDAY FIELD
COOPERSTOWN, NEW YORK

SPONSORED BY

Legends of Baseball

COLUMBUS, OHIO	CINCINNATI, OHIO
(614)488-1814	(513)271-3612

ROOKIE

ROOKIE

When Michael Jordan Came to the Minor Leagues

Jim Patton

Author of *Il Basket d'Italia*

▲▼ *Addison-Wesley Publishing Company*

Reading, Massachusetts   Menlo Park, California   New York
Don Mills, Ontario   Wokingham, England   Amsterdam   Bonn
Sydney   Singapore   Tokyo   Madrid   San Juan
Paris   Seoul   Milan   Mexico City   Taipei

Library of Congress Cataloging-in-Publication Data
Patton, Jim, 1953–
    Rookie : when Michael Jordan came to the minor leagues / by Jim Patton.
        p.   cm.
        ISBN 0-201-40959-3
        1. Jordan, Michael, 1963–   . 2. Baseball players—United States—Biography.   3. Basketball players—United States—Biography.
        I. Title.
        GV865.J66P38   1995   94-45956
                                                                    CIP

Jacket design by Jean Seal
Text design by Diane Levy
Set in 12-point Janson by Pagesetters, Inc.
1 2 3 4 5 6 7 8 9-MA-98979695
First printing, March 1995

Addison-Wesley books are available at special discounts for bulk purchases. For more information about how to make such purchases in the United States, please contact the Corporate, Government, and Special Sales Department at Addison-Wesley Publishing Company, One Jacob Way, Reading, MA 01867, or call (800) 238-9682.

To my father, James D. Patton, who departed far too soon.

Contents

Contents

Acknowledgments

Among the numerous people who contributed to this project, I'm especially grateful to Mrs. Lorraine Stauth, who came up with the idea of tracking Michael Jordan's season in the minor leagues; to my resourceful and indefatigable agent, Richard Pine, who pushed my proposal when every publisher in New York passed on it; and to Liz Perle McKenna, who finally took a chance on it (and on me) for Addison-Wesley. Special thanks to John Bell, whose editorial suggestions almost invariably won me over (no matter how long it took me to see the light).

My research—and the book itself—might have turned out deadly dull if certain people hadn't dropped a priceless story in my lap. My profound gratitude to David Falk, Barbara Allen, and several secretaries at Falk Associates Management Enterprises (FAME); and to Mike Barnett, Curt Bloom, Frank Buccieri, Terry Francona, Bill Hardekopf, Michael Jordan, and Chris Pika of the Birmingham Barons.

I couldn't have made it through the summer without the hospitality and generosity of my mom, Grace Patton, who long ago rated a lifetime service award, and of the matchless Mills family of Signal Mountain, Tennessee: Chuck and my sister Sarah, always supportive and generous and witty and wise; Katherine, teen *suprema*; and wildchild Lizzy Lou.

Acknowledgments

Several others in Signal Mountain helped make it a great summer for me: Phyllis "Me-Maw" Mills, Bill and Hilda Horton, Philip Tabb and his son Michael, Katie Connor, Monica Hertle, Sarah Kate Patton, and Mary Louise Roberts.

In Florida, my sister Rebecca and her upstanding husband, Bob Kable, provided the best in food, drink, and company, along with some blissful days out in the Gulf aboard *Yachts of Fun*.

All over the South, I was soothed and amused and inspired by my cassette-tape traveling companions: peerless vocal stylist the Reverend Al Green (who proved at Riverbend '94 in Chattanooga that even "How Can You Mend A Broken Heart?" can be a killer), and the incomparable Marvin Gaye.

I'm also grateful to the following individuals for encouragement and enlightenment and love over the years: Alberto Bortolotti, Jenelle Fleck, Randy Gardner, Mrs. Helen Krell, Dave Marlin (of course), Jeffrey Neuman, Terry Ross, Cameron Stauth, Jim Summers, Jim Taylor, and Tess Vigeland.

ROOKIE

For Sure,
Michael Means Business

*"The important thing is this: to be able at any moment
to sacrifice what we are for what we could become."*

— Charles Du Bos, *Approximations*

"BAG IT, MICHAEL!"

On the front of its March 14, 1994 issue, *Sports Illustrated* spanks its thirty-time cover boy, Michael Jordan, for his stab at a baseball career. The blunt headline is accompanied by a picture of Michael flailing pathetically at a pitch in the dirt.

The headline wasn't what longtime *SI* baseball writer Steve Wulf had in mind when, from his spring-training beat in Florida, he first discussed a Jordan article with his editors in New York. "I told them there were two parts to a story about Jordan. One was the resentment and animosity from major leaguers about what he was doing. The other was that he was working very hard, trying to be one of the guys, not being a prima donna."

The editors assigned Wulf the story. They talked about a headline like "Michael, Go Home!"—which, to Wulf, had a whimsicality that "Bag It, Michael!" lacked, and would have better reflected the tone of his story.

But "Bag It!" it is, with the subhead "Jordan and The White Sox Are Embarrassing Baseball," which obviously reflects the sentiment of the big boys at *SI*. The story inside is titled "Err Jordan" and features a full-page picture of Michael dropping a fly ball. Steve Wulf's text, it turns out, is only slightly more sympathetic.

Why are people so exercised about Michael trying baseball? Many think he's somehow disrespecting the game—that is, The Game. But baseball has survived the Black Sox scandal, Ty Cobb, racism, strikes, suspensions, drugs, Pete Rose, earthquakes at the World Series, and everything else imaginable. It will survive Michael Jordan taking a stab at it, no matter how he turns out.

Some decry Michael's tryout as a publicity or money-making stunt. But there are easier ways for a proud man to get publicity than by struggling with a difficult sport in full public view. As for money, twelve major corporations will reportedly pay Michael $31 million in 1994 for his endorsement. He's not hurting.

If the White Sox are willing to let him play, why should anyone object?

Even people who don't see anything wrong with Michael giving baseball a shot don't believe he'll stick around long. Either the Sox will send him home, or he'll get tired of his own futility, or he'll wake up some stifling morning in a cockroach-ridden room in some hick-town fleabag and ask himself, "What am I doing here?"

I disagree. Michael took his medicine in spring training, accepted an assignment to the Birmingham Barons of the Double-A Southern League, and is already getting a few hits in real professional games. This far into his adventure, he's not going to walk off. The cynics will only make him more determined.

To me, it's a most interesting study. What can an athlete like

For Sure, Michael Means Business

Michael Jordan accomplish in a game like baseball, picking it up at this late date, at this level? ESPN asks the retired pitcher Mike Marshall, now a professor of kinesiology and a college coach, which of Michael's basketball skills might transfer to baseball. "All skills are highly, highly specific," Marshall says, "so I'd say none. There's nothing in basketball similar to swinging a bat. I'd say that becoming a major-league hitter of quality is a three- or four-year, concentrated, day-in-day-out effort."

Sounds grim. But how fast might *Michael* be able to do it? I've paid less and less attention to baseball, my first love, in the last few years, but I've been reading the spring-training reports on this, watching the clips on *SportsCenter*, giving it a little thought.

A little. Mostly I'm fretting about my life—like what I'm going to do now that I've finished my book on Italian pro basketball and I'm not going to be able to pay next month's rent.

I'm sitting in my apartment in Portland, Oregon one afternoon in early April, fretting, when a friend calls and drops an idea in my lap: *Michael in the minors.*

And I think, *Yeah, I could do that.*

———

Not long ago I wanted to be finished with sports, quits with the whole business and everybody involved. I'd been soured by covering the NBA and the Dream Team, and by the general explosion of money and hubris in big-time sports over the last fifteen years, ten years, five—it keeps getting worse.

But I wound up in Italy covering a season in their pro basketball league, and the charms I'd once found (or imagined) in sports were rediscovered. In *athletes*, more accurately, because the games themselves had always been great. Italian pros aren't paid astronomical money and don't get interviewed very often and aren't asked to do advertisements—in short, aren't elevated to gods—so they don't behave as if they're gods and the rest of us a lower species. Dino Meneghin, *il monumento nazionale*, gave me his home phone number and invited me up to Trieste the first time we met. Roberto Brunamonti, the gentlemanly fourteen-year captain of the national team, actually seemed a little embarrassed about making his living in short pants—the first athlete who ever looked at me as if he wouldn't have minded switching places.

I made friends with a bunch of them. We shared long, wonderful meals; communicated as best we could; laughed. I traveled with teams—eventual *lega* champion Knorr Bologna and Korac Cup winner Philips Milano. A fine time was had by all, I think, and when I reluctantly came home, I wrote a happy book about the people and the experience.

I could cover Michael in the minors. The minor leagues won't be moneymoneymoney and gargantuan egos, but a bunch of guys fifteen to twenty years younger than me, scarcely more than kids, each praying he'll be one of the few to eventually move up to Triple A. The major leagues are still inconceivable to these guys. They'll be humble, approachable.

And Michael? I can't imagine he'll be too cocky, given that he's struggling with this difficult new game. Maybe he'll even be happy to share his day-to-day experience with someone who's decided that it's worth chronicling. Michael knows this is a unique experiment, turning an athlete like him loose on a new sport this late in his career, and he's got a keen sense of his place in sports history.

Covering Michael's summer would take me back. I was a big-time small-time pitcher once—that is, big-time in Little

For Sure, Michael Means Business

League, Babe Ruth League, Senior Babe Ruth, American Legion. I was a serious fan for years, well into the big-bucks era with its many distasteful aspects. I'm still a fan on the night of the All-Star Game (especially the pregame intros, with all the different uniforms arrayed down the first- and third-base lines) and during the World Series, even if I no longer look at every single major-league box score every single day of every season.

The thought of spending the summer in the Southern League arouses some of my earliest and happiest memories: summer nights in Southern minor-league parks with my uncle Doc when I was seven, eight, nine. I would visit him and Aunt Nellie in the tiny speck of Snow Camp, North Carolina after my Little League season ended up in Virginia. Doc was bigger than life to me: he was a scout for the Chicago Cubs, *a major-league organization*. He had autographed balls and media guides and stationery with the Cubs' logo, and closetsful of *SPORT* and *Sports Illustrated* and *The Sporting News*. He had radios on the big desk in the front room and on the nightstand in his and Aunt Nellie's bedroom *and* on the nightstand in mine, bringing in magical big-league games late at night from magical places like Cincinnati and Cleveland and Washington, D.C. Doc told me stories about famous sports people he knew, executives and coaches and players he'd signed who went on to the majors. But I most vividly remember the nights he took me to minor-league games in Burlington or Durham or Raleigh. It was the minors, yes, but a little kid just sees professional ballplayers, just like he wants to be. He's enchanted by the lights (he hasn't played a night game yet), the smells of hot dogs and cotton candy and whatall, the sounds of vendors and cheers and bat on ball and "Stri'THREEE!!!," the incredible size of the stadium, the gigantic crowds (probably in the hundreds).

I revisited the minors at fourteen, when my Babe Ruth All-

ROOKIE

Star team won the Virginia state tournament at Parker Field in Richmond, home of the Richmond Braves of the Triple-A International League. Even then the park seemed huge, with its full-size dugouts (real dugouts! below ground level! *pro!*) and distant fences and multilevel bleachers seating *thousands*. Even though they weren't too many years older than we were, the players we saw our first night in town seemed like serious grown-ups. Their girlfriends in the stands (mostly townies not long out of high school, I know now) seemed like serious grown-up women. The whole scene seemed bigger than life, though I knew by then that not all the players were destined for the majors. Somewhere along the line, I'd had the crashing realization that you didn't get to be a major leaguer simply because you wanted to be one.

Baseball stayed close to me even after a dead pitching arm ended my career when I was eighteen. For quite a few summers it was hard to believe I wasn't playing ball. Years after anyone looked at me and imagined a cocky, limber right-hander with a sharp curveball and pinpoint control, I remained that pitcher inside. Part of him remains yet.

You never lose interest completely. Something stirs in you when someone is putting together a great season or a great streak. There's still pleasure in realizing, say, that you're watching a true all-time great in the wondrous Ken Griffey Jr., or that Frank Thomas could become the most awesome hitter since Ted Williams—or Babe Ruth.

But baseball is blowing it this spring. It's got Griffey and Thomas and more young stars than it's had in years; it's rolling in money—yet they say there's sure to be a strike this season. Hard to love The Game.

I'm not in love anymore, but I could handle the minors. As recently as two years ago, I used to go out to Civic Stadium in

For Sure, Michael Means Business

Portland with some friends to watch the Beavers of the Triple-A Pacific Coast League. I enjoyed the games, of course, but I was more intrigued by the age-old stories of young guys passing through on their way up, of other young guys simply providing opposition, of older guys dropping back down on their way out of baseball. And of one memorable player who simply stayed: the Dominican outfielder and slugger Bernardo Brito ("BREEE-toe!!!"), the last of a dying breed, the career minor-leaguer blasting thirty to forty homers a year but never getting more than a brief call-up when major-league rosters are expanded in September. We'd sit in the left-field bleachers in the orange late-afternoon light, sipping cold ballpark beer while Bernardo sprayed us with batting-practice shots. We'd pick up hot dogs and move down behind third base when the sun dropped below the rim of the stadium and the faint chill set in. From there, the players soon distinguished themselves; we'd read their brief histories and professional stats in the program and wonder what would become of them. We all knew by now that only a few would ever reach the majors; fewer still would last, and maybe none would ever have us boasting, "We saw him before he was famous!"

The minor leagues are like real life. Throw bigger-than-life Michael into the mix and you've got something.

———

Trouble is, editors in New York aren't convinced that Michael will stick around long enough for there to be a book in it. Cautious types, they're happy to take the word of the cynics in the media.

It's astonishing that with all Michael accomplished in basketball, these tweedy geniuses—not to mention all the so-called experts in the sports press—don't have any better sense

ROOKIE

of him. He's obsessive. If he's not afraid of looking bad, as he proved the first day he came out for baseball, he's not going to be stopped by cynics. If nothing else, we know he's too image-conscious to let himself be remembered for giving baseball a half-assed shot and then walking off.

Steamy mornings in Chattanooga? One of my sisters lives nearby—nothing wrong with Chattanooga, with the mountains and the Tennessee River and Chickamauga and the Choo-Choo and the incredible aquarium. Memphis? Nashville? Jacksonville? Orlando? Not the glitz centers that Michael's used to, but hardly the outhouses of the U.S.

Reaching these venues, with few trips longer than three or four hours, the Barons travel in a luxury bus that Michael reportedly purchased for $350,000. It's got air-conditioning, six TVs, and extra legroom.

Musty hotels? The team stays at Holiday Inn, Ramada, La Quinta, Howard Johnson's, Hilton, Omni—no Ritzes, but a good step up from the fleabags of minor-league lore. Michael isn't suffering. They say he's even getting in his beloved round of golf every day, baseball or no, wherever he happens to be.

The so-called grind of daily baseball? Come on. It's a long season, yes, but it's a *game*. Anyone who enjoyed any success at all as a kid will attest that there's hardly a finer way to spend a summer than getting into the routine of playing ballgames day after day: the gradual, continuous education; the incremental improvement; the fresh chance to atone for the last game (as well as a new chance to fail). The camaraderie. The timeless smells of dirt and grass and leather and hot dogs and tobacco and bubble gum. The familiar feel of ball and bat and glove. Sunshine, dusk, darkness, bright lights. The absorbing, humbling, rewarding, hilarious game—who wouldn't enjoy it? Who couldn't at least tolerate it?

For Sure, Michael Means Business

The grind? Michael survived nine years in the grueling NBA.

On top of everything, he's got some new inspirational book coming out, *I Can't Accept Not Trying: Michael Jordan on the Pursuit of Excellence*. How would it look if he didn't stick this out?

No way Michael's going to walk off, and no reason to believe he'll be sent home. As the 1994 season moves into its second week, he's put together a nifty six-, seven-, eight-game hitting streak. We see him every night on *SportsCenter*, from some dimly lit park with signs all over the outfield fences. His swing doesn't look real good, and some of the hits are cheapos that happen to find a hole, but they're professional base hits all the same—more than a lot of people said he could do. Every hit will bring him back to the park.

And he's a happening. The Birmingham Barons received well over a hundred requests for media credentials for his first game—all the big-city papers plus NBC, CBS, CNN, ESPN, and TV stations from Germany and Japan. After games in Birmingham, the police have to stop traffic around the park so Michael can zoom off into the night. In other Southern League towns, fans are camping out overnight to buy tickets to Barons' games.

In Signal Mountain, Tennessee, outside Chattanooga, my nieces are ecstatic because my brother-in-law Chuck bought tickets, after the Lookouts announced they would move the outfield fences in by thirty feet to create thousands of standing-room spaces for the first Barons series. The girls don't know Michael Jordan from Magic Johnson (even my sister suspects there's a Magic Jackson out there, too), but Katherine and her thirteen-year-old friends want to go because it's a happening, the place to see and be seen for an evening; Elizabeth and the first-graders want to go because, even though they don't know exactly *why* all the clamor around this basketball player who's now playing baseball, they've been hearing "Michael Jordan" all their lives. His name has a life of its own, just as, say, "Elvis" did, or "Babe Ruth," and they want to be among the kids who can say they saw Michael Jordan in the flesh.

That's enough, just seeing him. Elizabeth calls me the day after the game. "We went to the game, Jimmy! We saw Michael Jordan!"

"Well, what did he do? How did he play?"

"Oh, he didn't play [turns out Michael sat out that game] but he was down there! We saw him in the dugout!" She'll be one of the coolest kids at Signal Mountain Elementary tomorrow.

Michael is *big*. In the first week of the new season, Michael—not Frank Thomas, not Junior Griffey or Barry Bonds or Greg Maddux—is on the cover of *Baseball Weekly*, with a three-page spread inside. His Upper Deck baseball card is worth more on the market than a Frank Thomas or a Barry Bonds. Demand is up ten percent for the kind of Wilson batting glove he wears, and Wilson is coming out with a Michael Jordan mitt.

———

Aside from the Michael-as-baseballer phenomenon, there's the persistent question of why he's out of the NBA, much less playing baseball. Many people weren't entirely convinced by the reasons he gave for quitting the Bulls last fall. Most likely he didn't wholly understand it himself, but maybe I can get some idea by hanging around him.

I don't know what to make of him, frankly. I think he was a regular guy once upon a time, back in Wilmington, North Carolina—one more young athlete trying to distinguish him-

For Sure, Michael Means Business

self. He came from a relatively stable middle-class family, unlike many NBA stars from inner-city, single-parent backgrounds. Even after he reached otherworldly status with his first NBA championship, I saw the residue of decency about him. I remember when he came to Portland with the Bulls the following season, how he arrived at the Coliseum and went to the trainer's room and hung up his coat (from a nifty green suit) and sat there on the bench and answered questions from a dozen reporters for twenty or thirty minutes, until we were chased out forty-five minutes before tipoff. He didn't say anything interesting—he was past the point, by then, where he could risk saying much—but he was smooth, impeccably polite, and looked directly at each questioner, fielding the insipid questions with grace.

Even hardened reporters stared at him as if he were an extraterrestrial, and when Michael looked at them he had the effect of a beautiful woman on men, dazzling them with mere eye contact. It doesn't matter what she says; the fact that she speaks to you is enough.

He was human, if little vanities are a giveaway. As the security cops hustled us away after the session, I asked Michael about his snazzy loafers. Alligator, he revealed with a little smile, seeming pleased I'd noticed.

Then he went out and destroyed the Trail Blazers, who were then at the top of their game.

During the Bulls-Blazers NBA finals a few months later, I met his father and mother and younger sister at a Nike bash in Portland. I spent twenty minutes with James Jordan, who I enjoyed immensely as he told stories and twitted us about the Blazers and spoke proudly of his boy. "You just enjoy it, ride the crest," he said of Michael's phenomenal success and the life they were all leading, "and when it's time for the ship to dock, you just hope you can say, 'Damn, we sure had a good time!' " I could see where Michael had come by his air of decency. I was impressed enough to go home and write my weekly column about James Jordan.

Michael became bigger than ever in mid-1992, as the Bulls whipped the Blazers for a second championship and the Dream Team destroyed all comers a couple of months later. At the Olympics in Barcelona, a Japanese reporter asked, "Mr. Jordan, how does it feel to be God?"

But his life has been pretty strange since then. During the third championship run, a friend of Michael's published a book (full of pictures of the two of them in good times) claiming Michael had lost more than a million dollars to him on the golf course (and wiggled out of paying most of it). During the finals against the Knicks, Michael boycotted the media after he was chastised for going to Atlantic City with his father the night before a game. The third consecutive NBA championship was anticlimactic.

Last summer his father, napping in his car on the side of a North Carolina road in the middle of the night, was murdered by a couple of idiot kids (allegedly) who threw his body in a creek bed. By the time it was discovered, the corpse was so decomposed it could only be identified through dental records.

Then came Michael's unexpected retirement, followed by the startling announcement of his new pursuit.

It was clear how big he'd gotten at the weird press conference to announce his retirement. Everyone was as shocked as they'd been when Magic Johnson, a year earlier, had called a retirement press conference. There was a huge crowd. Most of the Bulls were there, along with NBA commissioner David Stern, Nike guru Phil Knight, all kinds of heavyweights. But Michael was the man, dressed slicker than anyone else (as

For Sure, Michael Means Business

usual), in complete control—more than ever, right then, because he was doing what no one wanted him to do and there was nothing they (we) could rightly say about it.

Michael gave a considerable speech (959 words compared to Lincoln's 271 for the Gettysburg Address), saying what he thought were the right things. But it didn't come off just right. Michael kept referring to the press, a little nastily, as "you guys"—as in, "Hopefully I won't see too many of you guys in the future"—although he would later insist, over and over, that no one should think the press had driven him out of basketball. Clearly there were some hard feelings, and you almost wished he'd say, "The press *did* drive me out!" It would have been perfectly understandable, and might have moved the press to look at itself.

Michael said, much as they all say, "There's a lot of family members and friends I haven't seen because I've been very selfish in my career to get to this point and make sure I achieved all the dreams that I wanted to achieve. Now that I'm here, it's time to be a little bit unselfish in terms of spending more time with my family, my wife, my kids, and just get back to a normal life, as close to it as I can."

It didn't sound much like Michael, and it wasn't. We later learned that he had already decided to try baseball. He would go to spring training in February, and if the White Sox hired him into their organization he'd be away from home until September, at least.

Did Michael really know why he was quitting? For instance, it's easy to see how he *would* be fed up with the press. And he certainly knew they'd be waiting in every city, through another endless NBA season, to ask him about not only his gambling but also about his father's murder, reopening that grief every day.

ROOKIE

Anyone could understand why he needed to get out, if only for a year. Anyone could understand, and we could have more easily swallowed some honest emotion than the smug business of how basketball didn't challenge him anymore—how, in effect, he was simply too good to play with even the greatest players in the world anymore. After all, Picasso didn't quit art. Faulkner didn't quit writing. Ali didn't quit boxing. There was always something more.

Of course, the towering ego was probably a given, considering that Michael long ago had been elevated to god status—nearing God status, to many. Even President Clinton emoted on the deity's departure from pro basketball, "We will miss him—here and all around America, in every small-town backyard and paved city lot."

It took former Celtics great Kevin McHale to provide some perspective. "They said football would never be the same when Jim Brown retired in his prime. But it goes on. You people [reporters] won't believe this, but I guarantee you that in five years people will be saying, 'Michael who?' That's the way it is in this league. The names on the back of the jerseys change, but the league just keeps rolling on."

———

So why baseball?

One reason, surely, is that Michael's ego wanted him to go where none had gone before. "[My father and I] had seen Bo Jackson and Deion Sanders try two sports," he tells Ira Berkow of the *New York Times*, "and he felt I could have made it in baseball, too." Sure, Michael was the greatest in one sport, but he couldn't say he'd played two sports at the major-league level. The one way to trump Bo and Deion, and be the richest and the most famous *and* indisputably the most accomplished

For Sure, Michael Means Business

of jocks, would be to take up a new game at this late stage and actually make a major-league team.

And such things matter to Michael. Imagine the drive it took to reach those heights in basketball. He didn't want to be merely a very good player with loads of cash and toys; he wanted to be *the one*. He wanted the scoring title every year. He wanted the championships. After the Bulls' third in a row he reminded us that, while he couldn't match Magic Johnson's five titles, Magic had never won three in a row, so there. Michael had the snazziest wardrobe and the finest jewelry in the NBA. He and his wife were building a manor fit for a potentate, surrounded by a twelve-foot wall: a 29,000-square-foot house with tennis courts, shopping mall, launching pad. *Trump this, boys.*

He tells Ira Berkow he thinks about his father every day as he struggles with baseball. "He would say, 'Keep doing what you're doing. Keep trying to make it happen. You can't be afraid to fail. Don't give a damn about the media.' "

For all kinds of reasons, Michael will play this baseball season through.

Why *wouldn't* he? Beyond the challenge, and beyond what White Sox partner Eddie Einhorn calls "penance for his father's murder," there's the simple fact that Michael is a jock: playing games is what he does.

It's a story, if only one of these bright New York editors could see it. I'm primed for a summer of cruising the Southeast, watching minor-league ball (back to purity), seeing the sights—and seeing my mom in Atlanta, my sister Sarah and her family outside Chattanooga, and my sister Rebecca and her husband down in Florida. Time's a-wastin'. Michael is playing games, and I can smell the blooming lilac outside Mom's cottage in Patton Valley, up in the Smoky Mountains . . .

Double-Talk

*"One day everything will be well, that is our hope.
Everything's fine today, that is our illusion."*

—— Voltaire, *Poème sur le désastre de Lisbonne*

Birmingham Barons PR man Frank Buccieri is on cloud nine over Suzy Kolber's picture.

It all worked out: an editor bought my pitch, I borrowed $300 to drive cross-country, made it from Portland to Signal Mountain in sixty hours, called Frank down in Birmingham on Friday—and now here I am, on Monday afternoon, sitting in his cubicle in Hoover Metropolitan Stadium. Hoover is the bedroom community fifteen miles south of Birmingham that seduced the Barons into moving in 1988.

Frank, twenty-nine, is in his third year with the Barons, and his life has been different since the coming of Michael. "Lots of us have burned the midnight oil since this thing started, but everyone has loved it, even though we don't really come in contact with Michael very much. It's something you'll always be able to say you were involved with."

And the perks! Frank's got the look of love as he points to the black-and-white publicity photo of ESPN2's Suzy Kolber on his cluttered desk, signed, "Enjoy the attention!" "She's cute," I flatter him, and Frank, gazing at the glossy, says, "And this doesn't even do her justice. Doesn't do her justice at all."

Double-Talk

He picks a letter off the heap on his desk. "It's been pretty crazy. I must get twenty requests a day, all kinds of things. This one's from a high-school principal in south Alabama asking if they can bring their All-American football player to a game and get five minutes with Michael—for his guidance, his example."

Frank answers my next question before I ask it. "We don't do anything with these requests. Michael gets 2,500 pieces of mail a week—some come here, some to the White Sox, some still to the Bulls—but we just send everything on to his agent in Washington, D.C. It wouldn't be fair to Mike if we gave 'em to him. If he tried to do all these things, his life would be impossible."

Despite the Michaelmania engulfing Frank's life, his most significant contact with the man so far was a minute or so in Zebulon, North Carolina, on the first road trip. "I don't usually travel with the team, but we knew that first trip would be a circus. When we got over there a lady called from South Carolina asking if she could bring her sick mother up to meet Michael. I told her we couldn't promise anything. But they went ahead and made the three-hour drive up, and during batting practice the lady came down and asked if her mother could meet Michael. I went to Mike in the outfield with the request, and when he came in to hit he stopped by and said hello. A minute, minute and a half, no more, but it was all this old woman wanted. It's amazing how he affects people."

I guess so. I guess that's partly why I'm here. I explain to Frank that I've got a contract to write a book about Michael's season in the minors and I'm hoping to get a basic media credential to watch Barons games from the press box and go into the locker room afterward—the usual, whatever the average beat writer gets. I'll take it from there as far as establishing a relationship with Michael, setting up interviews, whatever.

ROOKIE

"Welcome aboard," Frank says. It's not his call—I'll have to clear things with the Barons' new media-relations director, Chris Pika—but Frank doesn't foresee any problems.

Unfortunately, Pika's all the way over in Greenville, South Carolina with the Barons for the next three days. Frank says Pika wouldn't normally travel with the team, either, but with Michael in the picture he's making every trip.

I tell Frank I'll chill at Mom's place in Atlanta for a couple of days, then meet Pika and the Barons on Thursday up in Huntsville. Will Frank please let Pika know in the meantime—ask him to ask the Huntsville people to leave a pass for me at the will-call window, and I'll catch up with him inside?

Done, says Frank.

He's so welcoming, so trusting, that I almost feel guilty somehow. Even though he hasn't asked for any ID or credentials, I hand over what I brought along: two of my old newspaper columns, one about Michael and the one about his father, along with a galley version of my upcoming book on Italian basketball.

"Enough, enough," Frank says. "Welcome aboard."

I stand up, thank him, shake hands, and leave him alone with Suzy Kolber's picture.

———

On Thursday morning, packed and ready to cut out of Atlanta for Huntsville, Alabama, I try calling Frank in Birmingham—Hoover, that is—to make sure everything is set up. I'm told he's at a meeting in town and won't be back for an hour, so I leave a quick message on his voicemail, "Heading for Huntsville. Will look up Chris Pika there."

And I cruise.

It's the South, sure enough. My little Honda doesn't have

Double-Talk

air-conditioning, and even here in April, even before noon, the sweat pops out on my forehead and my shirt gets damp in the time I sit waiting for a red light to change. The heat and humidity are going to be tough this summer. None of it bothered me as a kid growing up in Virginia, probably because it was all I knew, but after twenty years in cool, misty Portland, I'm not ready for this.

And if the weather doesn't tell me where I am, I know I'm back down South when, leaving a barbecue joint near Gadsden, Alabama after lunch, I hear a woman saying to an older lady in a wheelchair, "Ah got worried when we didn't see ya for a while—Ah was afraid you was *failin'*. " The older lady pats her friend's hand and reassures her, "Naw, honey, Ah ain't failin', but you're *precious* to ask . . ."

This is church country, of course, and a few miles up the road stands a huge, lonesome billboard: BIBLE OUTLET— THOUSANDS OF BIBLES UP TO 50% OFF.

It turns out that the sleepy burg of Boaz, Alabama has factory outlets for everything. SHOPPERS HEAVEN, declares the big Chamber of Commerce sign on the edge of town, and for a couple of miles there's nothing but billboards telling you where to find the South's (if not the world's) greatest bargains on clothes, boots, fireworks, firearms, you name it.

In the sweltering midafternoon heat I make it to Huntsville—"Rocket City," home of the U.S. Space and Rocket Center, which this week has opened a new exhibition commemorating the twenty-fifth anniversary of the first manned moon landing.

I locate little Joe W. Davis Stadium, and though it's more than three hours before game time, there's plenty of activity outside. I park my car in the lot, bring my notebook, and approach a drowsy young guy manning a gate. After hearing me out, he advises me to go up to the home team's second-floor offices and ask for someone named Patrick.

The Huntsville Stars' offices are abuzz with what seems to be a bunch of kids. The giddy atmosphere calls to mind a sock-hop planning committee or, more to the point, a high-school athletic department when the coaches aren't around.

A young lady points out Patrick, a doughy red-haired fellow in a red Stars polo shirt who's on his way out to the elevator. Even as I introduce myself, he breezes right past me. Tagging along, I tell him I'm supposed to locate the Barons' Chris Pika, but as I squeeze through the elevator doors after him he's shaking his head, *unh-unh*. Even after the doors close, he won't look at me. I repeat that I'm supposed to meet Chris Pika here, but Patrick just stares at the buttons on the wall as if he's never seen anything so fascinating, shuffling from one foot to the other, shaking his head, *nope, nope, nope*.

"Well," I ask as we get off the elevator downstairs, "do you know anything about it? Patton's the name . . ."

Still not meeting my eyes, Patrick nods. "Yeah, I know about you. I'm not supposed to give you a pass."

For a moment I think he's joking, but I know that kids like this don't tease grown-ups they've never seen before. (Actually, Patrick turns out to be twenty-four, and the Stars' general manager.) I tell him there must be a mistake. "*Jim Patton*. I have a contract to write a book about Michael Jordan in the minor leagues. I talked to the Barons' PR man the other day and I was supposed to meet Chris Pika here tonight."

Patrick finally looks at me—alas, much as he might eyeball vermin. "They told me not to give you a pass," he repeats.

"*Who?* Frank Buccieri down in Birmingham, or this Chris Pika?"

"I think it was Michael Jordan's agent."

Double-Talk

"His *agent*?" Since when does an agent have anything to say about media access in professional sports?

But there's no point in hassling young Patrick, who's just doing what he's told. I head out to my car and take off for Signal Mountain, two hours northeast, to ponder this at Chuck and Sarah's house.

———

Michael Jordan's agent is David Falk, widely known as one of the most important and loathesome men in the NBA world. Coming out of college Michael signed up with the ProServ agency, in which Falk was a partner, and went along when Falk broke off and eventually formed Falk Associates Management Enterprises (FAME).

Falk has benefitted from his association with Michael to the estimated tune of $5 million annually in recent years. He has also, by most accounts, developed a nauseating sense of his own importance. I never met him when I was covering the Trail Blazers, but I know that when the word "Falk" comes up, "arrogant" usually isn't far behind—and worse, although most NBA executives and agents fear Falk's wrath and stifle their epithets until a writer promises the conversation is off the record. A typical comment came from a team vice president who requested a promise of anonymity before telling me "David has this aura of respectability—he wears a tie and shakes hands—but he's one of the most shameless human beings I've ever met."

Not everyone is so worried about hurting Falk's feelings. In 1992, after Falk's client Xavier McDaniel left the New York Knicks for the Boston Celtics, Knicks president Dave Checketts said, "What my dealings with David ultimately prove is that the only rule is that there are no rules. When he has leverage, he will do anything."

Charlotte Hornets president Spencer Stolpen said, "When it comes to negotiating a contract, David . . . has great selective memory, and he often becomes bigger than the player."

Other agents resent Falk's success. Many represent players who've left Falk in the last few years, claiming he neglected them for Michael, such as Dominique Wilkins, James Worthy, Buck Williams, John Salley, Dale Ellis, and the late Reggie Lewis. Since these agents can't knock Falk off his perch for now, their only hope is that his own warped nature will do him in. "Falk is smart," one told me, "but his extreme arrogance makes him do stupid things."

Now, though I've never so much as spoken to him on the phone, I hear that Falk told the Huntsville Stars to refuse me a pass to a minor-league baseball game. Even more incredibly, they do what he says!

It's disheartening, even though I know Falk can't get away with it in the long run. I mean, I come to the minors because I can't handle the ego and greed in the big time, and this is what I find.

Agents. They used to be nonexistent, then became occasional, gradually became ubiquitous, and now a guy like Falk is shooting for omnipotent.

———

Friday morning I get on the phone. First, to the Southern League office in the Birmingham suburb of Trussville, which issues a message in the corn-pone drawl of longtime president Jimmy Bragan. "It's Thursd'y afternoon; Ah've got a doctor's appointment. Ah'll be back in here late—ya know how it is when ya go to a doctor's office. If at the tone ya'd leave a name and number, just as soon as Ah get back to the office Ah'll be happy to give y'a call. Thank ya. Have a good one." Sounds like a verbal Gone Fishin' sign.

Double-Talk

I call Frank Buccieri, the Barons' PR man who welcomed me aboard only a week ago. "What happened, Frank?"

"I told you we send all Jordan requests to Washington, D.C. We did let them know about you, and a woman named Barbara Allen at Falk Associates was supposed to take up the matter with Chris Pika."

"Well, they took it up, all right. In Huntsville yesterday a kid named Patrick looked at me like I had leprosy, and said that Jordan's agent said not to let me in. I never even met Chris Pika."

Frank, it's clear, wants to stay out of it. He says I need to take it up with Pika—who, he reveals now, is a bit of a stickler for credentials.

So . . . who's Chris Pika?

The Barons' media guide tells me all I need to know (to know I'm in trouble): the twenty-nine-year-old Pika, in his first year in the organization, is a career athletic-department flack. As an undergraduate he worked on the sports-information staff at Loyola College in Maryland, later joined the staff at George Washington University, and for the last five years has been the assistant sports-information director (SID) at the University of Alabama in Birmingham.

I never get along with sports flacks, who seem to thrive on reflected glory and develop an outsized sense of their importance. While covering the NBA I had a running battle with a couple of pallid jocksniffers who, having moved up the flack-ladder from high-school athletic department to college SID to the plum major-league jobs, wore soft Italian loafers and basked in their importance-by-association and flexed what little muscle they had at every opportunity. They reminded me of the nurses I knew during my years working the mental wards, who, because they were expected to kiss up to the doctors, turned around and expected the aides to kiss up to *them*.

ROOKIE

I can't relate. I can see falling into PR under some circumstances—if all else fails, say—but I hardly know what to make of people who grew up with that kind of ambition all along.

It's like growing up wanting to be an agent.

———

Chris Pika doesn't surprise me one bit when I reach him at the Marriott in Huntsville.

He says he's talked to Falk's assistant, Barbara Allen, a couple of times a day since Michael joined the Barons. Yesterday she faxed him saying that because Michael has no involvement with my project and publishes his own works through Harper-Collins, he "will not be available for an interview or to take any questions [from Jim Patton]." Pika passed the message to Patrick in Huntsville, which translated into my being denied a credential.

I keep telling Pika, to no avail, that I'm not asking for private time with Michael, not really asking anything at all of him—I merely want the basic access to the *team* that professional organizations traditionally grant reporters and journalists.

"You're not with a legitimate news service," Pika says, "which is why Huntsville didn't let you in and why I probably won't let you in in Birmingham."

"I'm writing a legitimate book for a legitimate publisher," I counter, but Pika insists I'm working for myself and that's *not* OK.

Eventually he suggests I call Barbara Allen myself. I figure that despite the bluster about what *he* will and won't permit me in Birmingham, he'll permit me whatever Jordan and his people will permit me.

This morning, Ms. Allen isn't in her office at FAME. I leave

Double-Talk

a message on her voicemail, though I don't expect to hear back from her.

On second thought . . . just to make sure she hears *me*, I send a rather heated fax. I do these things when I get indignant—can't help it.

Ms. Allen hears. "First, we didn't like the tone of your fax," she says when she calls back. "This talk about 'agents' manipulation and control'—let me tell you, we don't control the Birmingham Barons' media-access policies. As far as I know, a journalist with a project should get basic access to a professional team. If the Barons don't let you in, it's their decision." She adds, for some reason, "I showed your fax to Mr. Falk, and he just laughed."

Anyway, I let her lecture me for a couple of minutes. I sense she needs to know that *I* know FAME is big and I'm small, and then she'll bargain.

Finally she segues into her story of how busy Michael is, how he doesn't have time to sit for interviews with someone who wants to write his biography. I tell her I'm not writing a biography, but a pleasant little book about Michael's summer in the minors. I'm not asking for personal interviews; I just want to get basic access and hang around, keep my eyes open, talk to the other players and coaches, throw in a question to Michael now and then.

Not a biography? Ms. Allen seems to lighten up a little, and I can only wonder what other misinformation FAME has gotten about me from the boys in Birmingham.

Ms. Allen has quit acting tough now. Asking about my year in Italy, making small talk, she's almost human. At the end she repeats that as far as she knows, a writer with a project is normally credentialed by pro teams, and says she'll speak to Pika about me this afternoon. "And I'll mention this to

ROOKIE

Michael. He's probably at the ballpark by now, but he should be calling in before the game. If you're not trying to write a biography, I don't think he'd object to you being around."

"Tell him I'm not out to smear him. There's nothing to be afraid of."

"Oh, we're not worried about that. I have no fear of putting Michael together with any writer—I don't think there's any bad news there. But Michael doesn't think there's any story. People want to write his biography and he says he's too young, there's no story. People want him to talk about baseball and he says there's no story because he hasn't done anything yet."

"But," I say, "his attempt at baseball, the *process*, is an interesting story. And I don't need private interviews to write it. I only need the basic access that, as you said, legitimate journalists usually get in professional sports."

Rocket City

"To persevere, trusting in what hopes he has,
is courage in a man."

— Euripedes, *Heracles*

On Saturday I make the drive back down to Huntsville, where I'll pay my way in and watch my first Southern League game. I'll try to talk to Pika and see if Ms. Allen has cleared things up.

Cruising into Rocket City, where I see WELCOME MI-CHAEL JORDAN signs outside A & W and Sam's Country Kitchen Buffet and half the other eateries, I realize these minor-league towns take a kind of proprietary interest in Michael. The biggest of big-timers is *theirs*, at least for a while!

According to the *Huntsville News*, Michael knocked in the winning run on Thursday night with a double off the fence, his second extra-base hit of the season. Last night, in front of a record crowd of 12,819 at Joe W. Davis Stadium, he went 0-for-4 with two strikeouts, his average falling to .281. Meanwhile, the Chicago Bulls opened their Michael-less playoffs with a win over Cleveland as former second banana Scottie Pippen scored thirty-one points.

Out at the stadium I pay $2.50 for parking and, with the box seats sold out, $4.00 for a general-admission ticket.

It's a sweet spring evening, warm but not oppressive, perfect for baseball. The moment I walk into the park, the familiar sights and sounds and scents of baseball, the eternal rhythm and beauty of it all, take me back to Southern parks thirty-odd years ago, to Richmond's Parker Field in 1968, to Portland's Civic Stadium a few years ago. Fifty or sixty big signs line the outfield fences, advertising everything from McDonald's and Kentucky Fried Chicken to CableAlabama and all kinds of local businesses. The ushers, courtly Southern gentlemen who've been here for years, inquire "How're *yew* t'naht?" as they help you to a seat. Down on the greensward, the Huntsville Stars are taking batting practice in their red-white-and-blue; between pitches, a coach on one side of the batting cage slaps ground balls to the infielders, just as coaches have done down through the baseball ages. A former big-time small-time player is reminded how good it felt to make a nice snag on a grounder or a long fly, even in warm-ups, even for the thousandth time. Every so often you could imagine how it felt to be Brooks Robinson or Willie Mays. If you were lucky, you did it once or twice in a real game.

As the Barons, one and two and three at a time, emerge from their dugout and head to right field to loosen up, local TV crews out on the grass and a few dozen kids hanging over the railing next to the dugout await Michael's appearance.

He comes out last of all, politely sidestepping the reporters and loping out to join his teammates on the smooth outfield lawn. They huddle briefly around manager Terry Francona, then jog to center field and back before going through some agility drills.

When the Stars leave the field and the first Barons come in to start batting practice, the kids crowd the rail, ready to stretch out and thrust their balls and gloves and caps and programs into Michael's hand to be signed.

But Michael is seventh in tonight's batting order, meaning seventh in line for BP, and until it's his turn he stands alone out in right field. Most of his teammates are in twos and threes, but

Rocket City

Michael looks perfectly content—serene—and I remember how he used to say that in his mad existence the basketball court was the only place he could relax. He looks like a guy who savors a minute or two of quiet time, wherever he finds it.

I spot a pleasant-looking guy down on the field wearing a black Barons polo shirt, and when he comes up the aisle beside me I stop him and introduce myself. He's the radio man, Curt Bloom—thirtyish, with a deep announcer's voice and a friendly line of patter.

He points out Chris Pika down on the field: a dull-looking fellow with a premature potbelly and Deputy Dawg jowls, wearing khaki shorts and a black Barons cap. An insider—schmoozing now with a reporter, now with Barons first baseman Troy Fryman.

Curt Bloom heads up to the booth in the press box to do his pregame bit. When Michael finally jogs in from the outfield and picks up his bat, another couple hundred fans move down to the railing, parents exhorting little kids to "get up there and look at him real good!" The kids scream, "Michael! Please sign this! Michael! Michael! Michael!" but Michael's got them tuned out, or at least he's pretending he has.

An extra cop materializes and hovers within ten feet while Michael stands behind the cage swinging his black bat with a weight on the end.

Michael steps in to face Terry Francona's left-handed meat-balls at 5:41 P.M.—my first time seeing Jordan the baseball player in the flesh. With everyone in the park watching, in-cluding some curious Huntsville players lolling on the rail in front of their dugout, he drops a bunt toward third base and another toward first (in timeless baseball tradition), then pro-duces weak ground balls with his first two swings. But then, three times running, the fans roar when he cracks medium-long fly balls—all easy outs in a game, nowhere close to leaving

ROOKIE

the yard, but whose sound and trajectory provide a split second of excitement each time. They want to see him park one!

On his second round he hits some better shots, and finally one clears the left field fence. A cheer erupts—but a brief one, as if it suddenly occurs to everyone that they're cheering a batting-practice homer, and one that barely made it over the fence. It's really not very exciting, even if it is Michael.

The kids down close are yelling at him and vainly reaching out as Michael, head down, walks back to the dugout after his licks. "Wave to me, Michael, *please!*" two giggly teenage girls squeal. A thirtyish fellow tells me he moved to Birmingham from Chicago a few years ago. "I'm not a baseball fan, but I *am* a Jordan fan. My sister went to high school with his wife—I guess that makes us close enough!"

A beer vendor turns this way and that with his unwieldy cooler, delivering his shtick in a cheerful Louie Armstrong vocal: "Be-uh he-uh! Be-uh he-uh! Y'all bettuh get this be-uh before Ah disappe-uh! Get some be-uh while Ah'm in the atmosphe-uh!"

The girls who begged Michael to wave to them walk away pouting, "He could have at least looked at us."

On the field, in the thirty-minute lull between warm-ups and game time, a few Huntsville Stars play pepper—another baseball tradition unchanged through the ages. A few guys from each team stand at the railing, signing autographs for these worshipful kids. Who knows which player, if any, will ever make it out of the minor leagues?

The beer man, from some distance, teases "*Root* be-uh! *Root* be-uh!" Then, "*Free* be-uh! *Free* be-uh!"—and, when heads turn his way, "Over *they-uh!*"

Joe W. Davis Stadium gradually fills. Michael Jordan doesn't come to Rocket City every day. Thursday night, for the first game of the series, a local TV station split the screen on its regular programs every time Michael came to bat. Last night they televised the whole game, a first, and there was still a record crowd at the park.

Amazingly, no one ever comes for the box seat I appropriated for batting practice, and I watch the early innings with a sedate couple in their sixties who've had season tickets for years. They fondly recall the big-leaguers who've passed through Huntsville, including former Barons Robin Ventura and Frank Thomas. "And Walt," the woman says, looking at her husband as if she's referring to their beloved son. "Walt Weiss [now with the Florida Marlins] played here on his way to the A's. When you saw Walt play shortstop, you knew you were seeing the real thing."

The crowd is relaxed until Michael comes out of the dugout and starts swinging his bat in the on-deck circle in the top of the second inning. The noise starts. Flashbulbs start popping. People stream down the aisles for a closer look until the ushers draw the line.

When Michael steps in to hit, the crowd roars in anticipation. Tall and rangy, of course, he cuts a dashing figure: black batting helmet, black turtleneck, long black sleeves emerging from his grey Barons jersey, with black Wilson wristbands (the white "Wilson" script facing out just so) and black batting gloves on both hands. His grey pants are pulled all the way down, leaving no socks visible as they plunge into the hightop black Nike cleats at the ends of those long, slender legs. He swings a black bat. (And plays the field with a black mitt.)

He'd look great if he could hit.

This time it's over in one pitch: a sharp one-hopper back to the pitcher, who throws Michael out at first.

The Barons, however, proceed to jump on the Huntsville pitcher. Eight batters in a row hit, walk, or reach base on an error, so there's still only one out when Michael comes up

ROOKIE

again. The same roar goes up; the flashbulbs pop; the kids try to slip down the aisles for a closer look.

Michael slaps another grounder back to the pitcher—the only difference being that this time, with a runner on first, the result is a double play. End of inning.

But at least he's hitting the ball.

After the third inning the promotions begin, a highlight of minor-league ball. Two fans are called out of the stands to run the Dizzy Bat Race. On the grass between the first-base line and the dugout they take their marks, then take off on "Go!" for two Barons usherettes about thirty feet away, each holding a bat upright—fat end on the ground, knob up. The contestants bend over, place their foreheads on the knobs of the bats, and attempt to run tiny little circles *around* the bats . . . eight times . . . then, if they're still on their feet, run back to where they started. It's hilarious. One guy gets dizzy and collapses in a heap after four hunched-over orbits around the bat. The other guy completes the eight turns, straightens up, takes a few rubbery steps back toward the finish line—then promptly zooms off the wrong way and skids facefirst into the basepath between home and first, taking a mouthful of dirt and messing up the precisely chalked foul line. Meanwhile, as the usherettes help this poor guy to his feet, his opponent gathers himself and completes the course to win a certificate for dinner at a Subway sandwich shop. The good-natured loser gets a sandwich for taking part.

A half inning later, a little kid is called out of the stands to try to throw three balls through a hole in a signboard a few feet away: one strike wins a pizza at a local joint; two strikes, a pizza buffet for five people; and three, the buffet for twenty. This kid hunches over, squints at the hole like Nolan Ryan, and goes through an elaborate, much-practiced windup. He zings one, two, three balls right into the target, with panache. The crowd loves it.

Rocket City

Three quick outs in the real game, and the usherettes in their bright red Stars shirts are escorting two couples out of the stands for the Water Balloon Bust. As the PA man ticks off fifteen seconds, the pairs go at it: one partner tosses up water balloons as fast as possible while the other makes like Reggie Jackson. Who can splatter the most balloons in fifteen seconds? The Water Balloon Bust theme backs up the PA man's dramatic play-by-play as the contestants frantically *toss! smash! splash!* as fast as they can, *toss! smash! splash!* Everybody's drenched; everybody's laughing; everybody wins something. It's a hoot.

In the bottom of the fifth, with a Huntsville runner on base, the batter hits a soft liner to right field. Routine. Michael coasts over, seems to have it lined up—and drops it.

The miscue helps the Stars load the bases, at which point the scoreboard flashes the message that a grand-slam homer here means a free buffet at Terry's Grand Slam Pizza for everyone in five sections of the stands. Under normal circumstances, five sections wouldn't amount to many people, but Terry must be sweating right now at the prospect of giving away several hundred buffets.

He's reprieved when the next Star pops up to end the inning.

An inning later Michael shines out in right field. First he goes a long way toward the line to make a nice running catch. Moments later, with a Star on second base, he covers even more ground, and not only makes a sliding Roberto Clemente catch right on the foul line, but scrambles to his feet and pegs the ball to second to double up the base runner, who figured to score easily and is already around third.

It's a big-league play. Twenty-four hours later *SportsCenter*, which has twitted Michael the baseballer considerably, includes it on Sunday night's "Plays of the Week."

Birmingham, Alabama

*(in which his Michaelness
grants me a brief audience)*

*"The human being as a commodity is the disease of
our age."*

— Max Lerner, *The Unfinished Country*

I arrive in Birmingham, "Magic City," on Tuesday, May 3,
seeing signs like WELCOME MICHAEL JORDAN and
THERE'S AN 'AIR' ABOUT BARONS BASEBALL. The
man himself, whose batting average stood at .327 last week
after his early flurry, has skidded to .250 with only one base hit
in his last twenty at-bats. Last night he went 0-for-4 with three
strikeouts against Orlando.

But he's still Michael. The sports section in the *Post-Herald*,
one of two Birmingham dailies, features a color picture of him
posing before last night's game with Kenny Rogers, his son,
and Kenny's "friend," a good-looking brunette who looks to be
in her twenties.

There's also a piece in the paper about Michael's protracted
slump—which is probably less a slump than a matter of Michael finding his level after pitchers started throwing him
curveballs. Michael is predictable: "I'm happy with my progress, but I'm not happy where I am now. I've got to get back on
a hitting streak. This is tough, but I'm not discouraged."

Batting coach Mike Barnett balltalks, "We just want him to

Birmingham, Alabama

stay on an even keel, be consistent with his work habits and his approach. I'm not concerned with his strikeouts. I didn't expect him to come out and not strike out some. I think he'll cut down."

A few hours before tonight's game, I take I-65 down to Hoover and I-459 out to Hoover Metropolitan Stadium, park in the near-empty lot, and go into the offices looking for Chris Pika. I called yesterday saying I hoped to see a few games of this home stand, and though Pika was far from warm, he did tell me to come on out to the park this afternoon and we'd meet to arrange a pass for tonight, then go from there.

So here I am, and the lady out front asks my name and goes and repeats it around the corner, and a moment later Chris Pika comes out to greet me, faux-cheery and faux-businesslike all at once, huffing about his overwhelming problems as he leads me back to his cubicle in an office he shares with several others.

"So, let me get you that pass." He hands me a card he's signed that will get me down on the field during warm-ups— today only—and into the press box to watch the game—today only—but will not, however, get me into the Barons' clubhouse after the game. That is, not much chance of introducing myself to Michael and winning him over.

"This is it?"

"We think that's pretty good," Chris Pika says. "That gets you into the game."

"But I can't get into the locker room like everyone else."

"Everyone else doesn't get in. People covering the Barons or Michael Jordan for legitimate news organizations get in. You're working for yourself."

"I'm working for a publisher. Is that illegitimate?"

"You work for yourself, not a legitimate news organization.

ROOKIE

Still, the club is kind enough to let you come in and see a few games and get your background material for your book."

"I'm writing a book on the *season*."

Pika's shaking his head, *unh-unh* . . .

"So I . . . I . . . ," I stammer in disbelief, "I can't get a general-access media credential like any stringer from any backwoods weekly?"

Pika's still shaking his head, slowly, side to side, *no way*. "Because your project is unauthorized."

He doesn't want to talk anymore, and I'm not going to get anywhere. I head out to the field before I do something regrettable.

———

Birmingham is a town with a baseball past. Its teams have played in various incarnations of the Southern Association and the Southern League since 1885. I've already been told I need to visit Rickwood Field, which was built in 1910 (named after the team's owner, millionaire industrialist A. H. "Rick" Woodward, who had the park built) and closed in 1987. Everybody who was anybody played at Rickwood: Ty Cobb, Babe Ruth, Dizzy Dean. Long-ago Barons Burleigh Grimes, the old spitball pitcher, and third-baseman Pie Traynor went on to Hall of Fame careers; likewise Rollie Fingers and Reggie Jackson, who schooled here when the Barons were an A's farm team in the 1960s. Jimmy Piersall played here, as did Vida Blue, Campy Campaneris, and gone-to-seed Denny McLain.

Not to mention the Birmingham Black Barons and their illustrious opponents. The Black Barons were charter members of the Negro Southern League in 1920 and rented Rickwood Field during the white Barons' road trips. Satchel Paige pitched and entertained for the Black Barons for three years, and by the time seventeen-year-old Willie Mays led the team to the last Negro League World Series in 1948, Rickwood had seen all the black stars from Buck Leonard to Jackie Robinson.

The oldest ballpark in America, Rickwood's been empty since 1987, except for the filming of the movie *Cobb* in 1993. There's a movement on to have it refurbished and used for local leagues, maybe the College World Series—keep it around, keep the memories alive.

Since 1989, a year after spanking new Hoover Metropolitan Stadium lured the Barons' previous owner out of Birmingham, the team has been owned by Suntory International, a Japanese conglomerate that produces pharmaceuticals at home and operates restaurants and wineries in the U.S. It's Suntory, by the way, that's raking in the unexpected monies from ticket sales and concessions this year, not the White Sox.

Hoover Stadium, which in its brief history has been home to White Sox prospects Frank Thomas, Robin Ventura, Alex Fernandez, Jason Bere, and Wilson Alvarez, is a good-sized minor-league park, with a capacity of 10,800. As in all minor-league parks, the outfield fences are covered with advertising from foul pole to foul pole—in this case, nearly sixty eight-by-twenty-foot signs, each of which brings the Barons $3,450 per season.

Just beyond the right-field foul pole—Jordanland, coincidentally—a basketball hoop on a backboard marked "$5000" stands beside a Mello Yello soft-drink sign. Five thousand dollars to any Baron who deposits a home run through the hoop. So far it's never been done.

In the Long-Lewis Ford Truck sign on the left–center-field fence, there's a real pane of glass in the picture of the truck—a new Explorer to any player who shatters it.

Advertising everywhere. Advertising pays the freight in the

ROOKIE

minor leagues, where the franchises don't have the TV deals or the volume of ticket and concessions sales that big-league teams have. The on-deck circles are sheets of blue plastic hawking Roebuck Mazda in white.

Up in the press box I meet Wayne Martin, Barons beat writer for the *Birmingham News*, the other daily paper. "Everyone who comes to town for Jordan," he chuckles, "someone tells 'em to talk to the old grey-haired fella." A friendly man in his fifties, born about forty miles south, Martin saw Willie Mays in Birmingham in 1948 and has seen most of 'em since. The singer Charlie Pride, he says with a smile, pitched for the Black Barons in the course of his first career; playing for the Louisville Clippers of the Negro Southern League in 1954 when the team's bus broke down, Pride was hastily sold to Birmingham for the price of a new used bus.

Michael has been as pleasant as any, says Martin.

"The day after his first game here, the kid who had pitched for Chattanooga came over to the Barons' dugout and said to Michael, 'I'm really embarrassed about this, but I wondered if you'd sign this ball for me.' Michael looked at him kind of hard and said, 'You're the guy who threw at me,' and the kid looked real uncomfortable. Then Michael said, 'You also struck me out twice.' But then he made a joke and signed the ball; the kid was relieved . . . "

According to Martin, Michael's young and unknown teammates seem comfortable with him. The joshing goes both ways. "The first thing I heard him say to another minor leaguer down in spring training was to a tall black kid who also was a basketball player and even resembled Jordan: 'Let's see you jump and touch the top of that wall, motherfucker.' The kid said, 'Let's see *you* touch it.' Michael just laughed and said, 'I know I could do it if there was a crowd cheering.' "

Birmingham, Alabama

I wind up watching the game with a pleasant guy in his mid-forties named Vern Gambetta, a former college track-and-field coach who went to work as director of conditioning for both the Chicago Bulls and White Sox organizations back in 1984, the year Michael arrived in Chicago. For the last few years he's worked exclusively for the Sox, mostly with the minor leaguers. He spends the summer in rental cars and Marriotts in Birmingham and Nashville and Sarasota and South Bend and Woodbridge, Virginia and Hickory, North Carolina, tracking prospects' conditioning and performance, designing workouts and therapy programs, doing a little coaching where he's qualified.

Vern is acquainted with Michael from his own days with the Bulls. He says he was surprised when Michael recognized *him* down in spring training a few months ago, after several years, and came over and said hello. He tells an anecdote about Michael taking time to sign a couple of posters for his children at the end of one of the star's early seasons with the Bulls. "After that I just thought, Man, you've got your number one fan for all time, because with all the people after you, you come and ask me if I brought those posters. I was really impressed as to what a genuine nice guy he was, and I've been his fan ever since."

Is Vern working with Michael on this trip?

"Not really. We talked a little yesterday—some stuff about running, some stuff about conditioning. I wanted to make sure he understood the need to do his legwork, and what kind of work he needs to do."

What does Vern think of M. J. the baseballer?

"I don't know if he'll become a star, but he'll succeed. The problem is that time isn't on his side. But he's made tremendous improvement from February until now. He listens, he really internalizes instruction, and I think that's what separates the immortal from the mortal, the great from the good. And he intuitively knows what he has to do to keep getting better. Every year he kept getting better as a basketball player, and if he had kept playing I think he would have *kept* getting better, finding different aspects of his game to improve."

There's not much of a crowd tonight, but those in attendance are nuts about Michael. He gets cheers in the first inning for fielding a routine single to right and flipping it in to second base.

They're on the edge of their seats when he comes to bat in the bottom of the second. But it's over in a moment, as Michael goes after the first pitch and lifts a harmless pop-up to short left.

But these 2,859 souls are on hand for Michael's greatest baseball moment so far. With the bases full of Barons in the fourth, he goes after the first pitch again and jolts a shot down the left-field line that rolls into the corner for a double and clears the bases. The fans, needless to say, go ape, and even a doubter thinks, *Gee, he looked good doing that,* just as he looked good making the Clemente-like catch and double play in Huntsville the other night. *If he could do that all the time . . .*

Of course, *anyone* who could do it all the time would be a major leaguer. And Michael is far behind his Southern League brethren in terms of instinct and technique, if not in natural talent, as he illustrates even before the roar from his two-bagger dies down. With the Orlando Cubs' pitcher in the stretch position before his first pitch to the next batter, Michael bolts for third—jumps the gun, that is, and the pitcher simply steps off the rubber and throws him out. Blunder!

"He didn't get a walking lead," Vern Gambetta says. "He's got to learn the walking lead, where he gets in motion but without committing himself. That time he went from stationary to full speed, and look what happened."

Michael looks defensive at the plate. He's prone to going after the first pitch, the sign of a hitter who fears he might need three swings to make contact and won't let any strike pass peaceably.

In his last two at-bats, Michael strikes out and flies out. After the called third strike he's moved to beef the umpire's call, and he keeps it up on his way out to right field until Terry Francona and Mike Barnett intervene. Since you don't see much strenuous arguing in the minor leagues, where the outcome of a game is next to meaningless, you've got to assume Michael's batting slide has him extremely frustrated.

———

When I reconvene with Chris Pika in his cubicle the next morning, two hours before the midday "Businessman's Special," he again concedes me pregame and press-box access—for today—but no locker-room entry. No Michael.

I'm miffed. I'm sick of these middlemen. Michael is such a regular guy, right? He's James Jordan's boy, the James Jordan who cheerfully told me that when he married Michael's mother Deloris "we had nothin', and no place to put it." He's an honorable guy from Wilmington, North Carolina, who wouldn't squeeze out someone who's been hired to do an honest job of work.

I head down to the field. I'm not one to disturb athletes at work—I figure the field or court is their space—but if the authorities won't let me get near Michael any other way, I'll try to catch him and present my case out here.

Most of the Barons are out starting to loosen up, but no Michael yet.

ROOKIE

But a moment later, standing in the grass behind home plate contemplating my situation, I spot him down in the left-field corner, coming through the gate from a covered, fenced-in area where he parks his fine cars. Dressed in loose-cut jeans and a knit shirt and carrying a basketball, he comes down the left-field line toward the infield in his comfortable, self-possessed walk . . . looking up at some people calling him from the stands, bestowing a smile . . . looming larger as he nears third base, coming my way.

I take a few steps toward third, placing myself in his path and eyeballing him as he comes closer.

Michael notices. He's within ten feet and giving me the eye when I step up and venture, "Michael? Can I talk to you for a minute?"

"Your name?" he inquires, not breaking stride.

I tell him, and before I can go further a look of recognition crosses his face. "I've heard about you," the famous voice says as he moves past me. "Unauthorized, huh?"

Jesus.

He's moving away, headed for the Barons' first-base dugout, and since he didn't answer the first time I merely repeat myself. "Michael? Can I talk to you for a minute?"

"Don't have time now," he flings over his shoulder, bopping on through the dugout on his way to the clubhouse. I take it to mean he'll never have time.

Unauthorized. A buzzword, rife with ugly connotations, and I'm getting a whiff of someone having floated it into this situation.

Hmmm . . .

Fifteen minutes later, as the Barons go through stretching exercises out in right field, I spy Michael, in uniform now, listening to Vern Gambetta down in the corner. Vern's showing him something about keeping his balance while taking a lead off base. I stroll down the right-field side, thinking I'll just hang around nearby—I've got no intention of approaching Mister Man again.

A minute or two later, Vern moves on and Michael starts stretching with the others.

And not thirty seconds later, to my surprise, Michael sort of sidles over to where I'm loitering and—still stretching, not even making eye contact, as if he'll handle me with three percent of his attention—says, "So what about this book?"

Feeling as if I've been granted an audience with the God-father and have fifteen seconds to make my case, I hurriedly explain that I intend a simple book about his summer in the minor leagues and about minor-league ball itself; I'm not asking for private interviews if he doesn't have the time or inclination; I'd just like to join the other reporters in the clubhouse after the games and talk to his teammates and maybe occasionally ask him a question or two; but the Barons won't give me clubhouse access without his approval, and are threatening not to give me any access at all after this home stand.

Suddenly Michael's cool. I know he's been told I'm one of those "unauthorized" guys, but in person anyone can see I'm harmless. Actually looking at me now, Michael shrugs and says, "It's OK with me. As long as you're writing about baseball, and it's not about what I'm doin' when I'm not playin' baseball . . . If you want to be there with the other reporters asking questions about baseball, it's OK with me. I've got to talk to the reporters every day anyway."

Bingo. He said it. *Him.*

I thank him. "Can I tell Chris Pika you said OK? He keeps telling me I need your approval."

ROOKIE

Already moving away, Michael chuckles. "Naw, I'll tell him. He wouldn't believe you."

He's right. He's nice to think of it.

Bingo! I knew it: cut out the middlemen, the layers of agents and flacks and bodyguards and yes-men, and you've got a chance. Michael's OK. He heard me out and, finding nothing sinister, gave me his blessing. Didn't even bring up "unauthorized" again.

I guess I'm authorized now. Encountering Pika as I stride back toward the infield, I can't resist telling him what Michael said. "We'll look into it," he harrumphs, hurrying by as if he's got all sorts of bigger fish to fry, but what's there to look into? Michael said OK.

It's going to work out. Five minutes later, from my press-box seat, I see Michael call Pika over and talk to him for a minute or two.

Yeah, Michael's all right, if you can only get to him through all the middlemen.

Spotting Barons president Bill Hardekopf up in the press box a few minutes later—who, Pika's assured me, has been in on the conversations about my "situation"—I decide to try to straighten things out with him. Can't do much worse than I'm doing with Chris Pika.

Sure enough, Hardekopf knows who I am, and I can tell he doesn't like whatever he thinks he knows about me. But what can I do? "I keep getting put off," I explain, "because I didn't get Michael's permission to write a book about him. I never thought I *needed* his permission. But I talked to him a few minutes ago and he said it's OK with him if I'm around. He said he'd pass it on to Pika, and I just saw them talking down there."

Clearly not convinced, Hardekopf says he'll talk to Pika. "If

Birmingham, Alabama

it's OK with Michael," he allows, "that might open up a few things for you."

If it's OK with Michael. "Do you think I'm lying?"

Scanning me up and down with a skeptical eye, Hardekopf says, "Anyone could come in here and say they're a writer."

I almost laugh out loud. Sure anyone could, but why *would* they? To watch some minor-league ballgames for free?

I tell him I've identified myself to his people every possible way except fingerprints, and if Pika hasn't shown him my old columns or the galley copy of my Italy book, that's between him and Pika.

"We'll see," he says. "I'll talk to Chris. A few things might open up if Michael approves. But," he stresses, "we've got to get Michael's and Mr. Falk's approval."

So. So much for the mystery of who's making the calls here.

But Michael said OK. Directly to me, up close and personal. *It's OK with me. I've got to talk to the reporters every day anyway.*

All things considered, I'm feeling pretty good.

———

Two school-busloads of Shelby County kids, sitting in a block of seats far down the right-field side anticipating a close-up view of Michael in the field, are disappointed when the lineups are announced: Michael is the Barons' designated hitter today. Not only will the kids miss the close-up view of him in the outfield, they're too far away from home plate to get a good look at him at bat.

But it's another sparse crowd (3,952 announced, a white lie), and by the time Michael steps up in the first inning the kids are drifting down to empty seats nearer the plate. They see their man take a fastball right down the middle for called strike three. In the third he fouls out weakly to the first baseman.

ROOKIE

In the fifth he lines a solid single to left. Leading off first base, he's not only up on his toes but bouncing weirdly up and down, actually leaving the ground. Vern Gambetta's aghast. "We talked before the game about how you can't take off from a dead stop, you need a little movement before the pitch, but not *that*. If you're up in the air, you can't stop or change direction or do anything—you're at the pitcher's mercy."

But Double-A pitchers aren't that refined. Michael actually gets a good jump trying to steal second, and would probably have made it, but the batter swings and whacks a long, high fly to right, possibly headed out of the park. It doesn't make it, but it does clear the right fielder's head and should easily score Michael—except that Michael inexplicably pulls up between second and third, apparently thinking it's either a homer or it's going to be caught, and then has to hold at third when the fielder plays the ball off the fence and pegs it in.

Another sign of Michael's inexperience. But that's what the minor leagues are for.

Michael Loses His Jewels

"I detest that man, who
hides one thing in the depths of his heart,
and speaks forth another."

— Homer, *Iliad*

Thursday evening is so sweet and I'm in such a good mood arriving at Hoover Metropolitan Stadium, knowing I'm in with Michael, that I'm not even fazed by having to wait at the will-call window for fifteen minutes for the pass Chris Pika promised to leave for me.

I lean against a wall, my face tilted up toward the sun, eyes closed behind my shades. A couple of times I glance up to see the lady behind the glass eying me suspiciously—she didn't recognize me and knew by my non-accent that I'm a fer'ner—but by the time she and the man at the next window have made three or four calls trying to run down Pika, they seem grateful for my forbearance. I giggle when I hear an impatient voice over the PA system inside the park: "Chris Pika, please get up to the will-call window now. A guy named Jim Patton has been waiting for fifteen minutes!" When I start jotting notes about an unrelated flight of fancy, the woman asks very kindly, "Sir, are you writin' "—*rottin'*, she says—"about how long you're havin' to wait for your pass?"

I laugh. Ah *lahk* the hospitality down here.

ROOKIE

Where I find it, at least. Pika never appears, but he or someone eventually hands my pass to the woman behind the glass. I accept it with her apology and smile and head for the ticket-takers at the entrance. My pass still doesn't include locker-room access, but that's all right; the way these people work, it might take a couple of days even after Michael's OK.

It's a perfect seventy degrees at 6 P.M., the gentlest of breezes blowing as I come through the turnstile and pass the concession stands and the girls selling programs and emerge on the mezzanine to take it all in: the freshly mowed grass down below; the signs; the big scoreboard in right-center; the bleachers; the ballplayers, ushers, reporters, kids and parents filtering in. I take a seat down near the Barons' dugout on the first-base side.

As the sinking sun slants in over the rim of Hoover Stadium directly behind home plate, shading the infield and bathing the smooth green outfield in a gentle orange glow, a dozen Huntsville Stars run sprints in front of the left-field fence while the others finish up batting practice. In front of the Barons' dugout, number 30 (Kevin Coughlin, my program says, left-handed outfielder) plays catch with a couple of little batboys. A passing usherette in her fifties says, "Good evenin'," and I can't resist chatting with her, thinking, *There really is something to that good ol' Southern hospitality.*

I walk over to check out the Orioles, tonight's "Field of Dreams" Little League team, who are dressed in their uniforms (orange and black, like the big-league Orioles) and clustered along the first row on the far side of the Barons' dugout. At every game here a local team is invited to join the Barons in the dugout just before the game, where the youngsters collect autographs or simply gape at the bigger-than-life pro ballplayers. As each Baron is introduced and jogs out to his position, the kid or kids who play that position sprint out after him and stand beside him during the national anthem. Usually a few words are exchanged between tall and small—a joke, a high five. You can imagine the thrill for the young right-fielders.

The Orioles are a friendly bunch of nine- and ten-year-olds, clearly bent on getting a certain autograph on as many objects as possible this evening. One boy has three new balls jammed into his glove. His buddies have got balls, gloves, caps, bats, cards, posters, magazines, programs, and more.

"Who plays right field?" I ask.

"I do," says a freckled lad even smaller than the others.

"Lucky, huh? You get to stand out there with him?"

"Yeah!" the kid exclaims, mocking me for the excitement I faked for *him*. "Want my autograph?"

Smartass. But a smart kid: *he's* not in a swoon over the prospect of proximity to Michael.

Then again, for all his cool he's got two brand-new balls in his glove—reserved, I suspect, for a particular autograph.

A half hour before game time, with the Barons having warmed up and retired to their clubhouse, energetic Huntsville manager Gary Jones finishes off the Stars' infield practice by giving each man one last ground ball and producing a perfect sky-high fungo for his catcher. The Stars then give up the field to three young black men in Green View Lawn Care T-shirts, who perform the eternal ritual of raking the mound, dragging and hosing down the basepaths, and painstakingly laying the chalk lines for the batter's boxes and baselines. More kids come down to the front rows, anticipating the players' return, and threaten to crowd out the local TV crews at both ends of the Barons' dugout. Yet it's all quite peaceful, quite dreamy, as the orange light fills the park and amiable Southern

ROOKIE

voices drift around me and Dire Straits' "Money for Nothing"—which reminds me how lucky I am to be doing this for a job—segues into the ebullient "Walk of Life" on the PA system.

It's all going to work out. They can't keep me down, these Falks and Pikas and Hardekopfs. Especially not when Michael said OK.

When the Barons return to the dugout a few minutes before game time, manager Terry Francona comes out and stands at the mesh screen behind the plate, chatting with a cluster of kids. Francona, thirty-five, is the son of former big-league third baseman John "Tito" Francona (one of the first baseball cards I ever owned, back around 1960) and played ten years in the majors himself, batting .274 in 708 games. Last season, his second as a minor-league manager, he guided the Barons to the Southern League championship and was named *Baseball America*'s Minor League Manager of the Year.

Now, as he talks with a woman who's holding a baby in her arms and appears to be his wife—they look as if they're talking about grocery shopping, or who's dropping the kids at the pool tomorrow—a lively guy around forty comes down the aisle and calls, "Hey, Terry, was Tito Francona your old man?"

Francona breaks off his conversation and looks squarely at the fellow. "He's my *dad*," he emphatically corrects him, but then, seeing the guy isn't challenging him, adds pleasantly, "Not my 'old man,' but yeah, he's my dad."

"Well, he was a fine ballplayer," the man says. Francona thanks him, and the guy heads back up to his seat. (I'll bet he had Tito's card, too.)

Moments later, the woman I figured for Francona's wife arranges some kids in the seats in front of me and then comes up the aisle with the baby in her arms, probably heading for a bathroom. I stop her, introduce myself, explain my project.

Michael Loses His Jewels

Her name is Jackie. She and Terry met at the University of Arizona, where Terry was the College Player of the Year in 1980. They've got four kids by now. Terry, of course, has been away from their home in Tucson since spring training opened in February. This is a quick visit for Jackie and the kids, who will stay home until the end of the school year, then join Terry in the Birmingham apartment until school starts again.

I ask her what it's been like for Terry, having Michael Jordan as one of his charges.

"Well, Terry played in the big leagues, so it hasn't been such a big deal to him; it wasn't like he hadn't been around big stars before. From the beginning, he just wanted to make the situation as normal as possible for everyone involved. And for the most part, it has been."

We chat a minute longer, until she *has* to get the baby to a bathroom. Before she gets away I ask her what ever happened to Tito Francona. I half expect him to be long dead and gone—after all, he was a grown-up on a baseball card before I was old enough to fathom the numbers on the back—and it's a shot of middle-aged perspective when Jackie says he's about sixty now (only!), working for the park service up in Pennsylvania.

The PA man introduces "Babe Ruff, the most famous mascot in the South"—a guy in some doofy-looking, floppy-eared, big-foot dog outfit. The little Orioles take the field with the Barons, the anthem is sung, the kids run back in, and the game begins, with Michael dropping the leadoff man's routine fly ball to right.

I'm watching from a first-base box seat—a better spot than the press box on an evening like this—when who should tap me on the shoulder but Chris Pika.

And suddenly he's making nice. He apologizes profusely for the delay at the will-call window. I can't manage more than a barely civil "OK" before going back to writing notes in my tablet. When he asks if there's anything he can do for me, I shake my head. When he attempts some small talk, I shrug, still scribbling. Let him squirm.

"Oh, by the way," he finally says, as civilly as *he* can manage given his feelings about *me*, "I got a message today for you to please call David Falk in Washington, D.C. tomorrow. At your convenience."

So. I guess Falk has finally come to his senses.

———

Suddenly part of the In Crowd—I think—I feel more comfortable going up to the press box than I did the last two days. I make myself a sandwich, pick up some game notes, and sit down with Vern Gambetta.

"I told him he's got to go 4-for-4 today so he can work on his baserunning," Vern says when Michael comes to bat for the first time. A moment later he muses admiringly, "He'll get it. I was always amazed by the way he pays attention and absorbs every little thing. I wish we could teach that to all our young players."

Michael makes a start toward 4-for-4 by tagging a long fly ball to right center—not a great-looking swing, and the result isn't a blast, but it falls precisely between the right and center fielders and Michael coasts into second with a double.

He picks up some baserunning experience in the third inning. After beating out a grounder to shortstop for a single—making it speedily down the line in a very few, very long strides—he lights out for second on the next pitch but has to pull up when the batter swings and connects. It's a pop-up to short centerfield. Michael hesitates uncertainly near second base; then, as the ball drops in, he not only rounds the bag but recklessly bolts for third—only to think better of it, screech to

Michael Loses His Jewels

a halt, and dive back into second barely ahead of the throw from the alert outfielder, a twenty-two-year-old with infinitely more baseball experience than Michael.

More education: the next Baron hits a routine fly to center field, deep enough for Michael to tag up and move to third after the catch—except that, instead of getting back to second and tagging up as he waits for the ball to land in the fielder's glove, Michael hovers off the bag for too long, gets a late start for third, tries for it anyway and winds up dead by ten feet. He's got speed, but not the kind that outruns gaffes like that one.

It's a pleasant night at the park. In the Water Balloon Bust, sponsored tonight by Subway, one teenager splatters sixteen balloons in his fifteen seconds, missing two in the hilarious hurryhurryhurry of it all; the other guy promptly splatters seventeen in a row, to great applause, and wins "Buy one, get one free" coupons for everyone sitting in his section.

The mood is light in the press box, too. Barbecue, baked beans, cream pie. Vern Gambetta. The beat writers, Wayne Martin of the *News* and Rubin Grant of the *Post-Herald*; the organist, official scorer, scoreboard operator, PA man, sound man, stat man—mostly guys in their twenties and thirties, familiar, passing the hours of yet another game with tired jokes and bad puns and cracks about the players. Curt Bloom, the thirty-one-year-old "voice of the Barons," pops in from his booth between innings to snag some food or a soft drink. Hardekopf drops in and out, Pika, Buccieri, other Barons people.

I meet a fellow named Paul Hayward from England's *Daily Telegraph*, who came to Atlantic City for the Lewis-Jackson fight and then called his editor saying he wanted to come down and do an "atmospheric" piece on Michael in the minors. "People in England picture him playing in pastures, with a few

ROOKIE

people sitting in little wooden stands. I didn't imagine this."
How big is Michael in England? "Oh, he'd be as recognized in
High Street or in an English pub as he is in America. But the
baseball thing is unexplored. It's seen as whimsical." Is Paul
going down to the clubhouse afterward to try to get a few
quotes—since he, like all but one in this press box, can get in?
"I might. But I really don't need to, do I? He'll just say the
same predictable things, eh?"

I meet people from the Atlanta bureau of Japan's biggest
newspaper. A couple of reporters from Sweden are here. A
columnist from Baltimore.

Party time. Schmoozing. Pika's apparently forgotten that he
despised me twenty-four hours ago. "Just let me know ahead of
time when you want to come to games here," he says. All is
forgiven. We make like we've been buddies all along.

"Don't forget to call David tomorrow," Chris reminds me as
someone calls him away.

David.

———

Michael has lost something out in right field. After Huntsville
is retired in the sixth inning he stays out there looking around
in the grass for a minute or two, in vain, before heading in.
When the Barons go down, he trots back out and searches the
grass until it's time to play ball. After another three outs it's
clear he hasn't just lost a pack of gum: one of the umpires is out
there, the Barons' batboy, a couple of guys from the bullpen, a
few cops and ushers, plus Michael. No luck.

It's got to be his famous gold-and-diamond necklace, which
for some reason Michael wears on the field, though it's probably worth more than Liz Taylor's collection. It's surely the first
time such finery has been seen in the minor leagues, and I can't

Michael Loses His Jewels

help wondering if the other Barons still feel Michael is "just one of the guys"—these $1,000-a-month kids and Terry Francona and Sam Hairston, the sixty-nine-year-old coach who played in the Negro Leagues, joined the White Sox organization thirty-three years ago, and is probably still making peanuts.

The search party gets larger every half inning, commoners enlisting to help the potentate find his jewels.

When the necklace is finally recovered and Michael jogs in with it, he gets the biggest ovation of the night.

Meeting Mister Falk

"Little by little, the pimps have taken over the world. They don't do anything, they don't make anything— they just stand there and take their cut."

— Jean Giradoux, *The Madwoman of Chaillot*

Friday morning, I accept Vern Gambetta's offer to watch a couple of the young pitchers get videotaped at the American Sports Medicine Institute over at the University of Alabama in Birmingham.

Arriving at the Marriott to meet Vern, I find the two pitchers, Mike Heathcott and Al Levine, and the Barons' backup catcher, Rogelio Nunez, sitting on the curb out front. When Vern comes down, the four of them pile into his rental car, and I follow them to the campus in my wreck.

One side of the big room at ASMI is set up with benches and weights and exercise machines and mirrored walls. The other features an ersatz pitcher's mound at one end, a home plate at the other, and cameras and computer screens and technology everywhere. A few ASMI personnel quietly go about their high-tech business, including a guy up on a scaffold getting ready to film.

While the pitchers go through some stretching, I pick up a glove and throw a little with "Nunie." Vern asks if he should put the radar gun on me. Nunie says I should come out and pitch batting practice for the club. He doesn't know I won't be able to lift my arm for three days after this.

Nunie is a good-natured Puerto Rican in his sixth pro season, 24 this very day, with a great arm but a weak bat. One of the few married Barons, he nonetheless shares an apartment with a teammate like most of the others; his wife stays back home during the season. Nunie rooms with outfielder Scott Tedder, who was the 1988 Division III college basketball Player of the Year, averaging 29.5 points per game for national champion Ohio Wesleyan.

Al Levine, a twenty-five-year-old from Chicago who's one of the Southern League ERA leaders so far, is another of the half-dozen married Barons. Al, in his fourth pro season after playing college ball at Southern Illinois University, says he would never choose to live in these parts—"Too hot, nothing to do"—but he brought his wife along for the summer and they're tolerating it fine. They've got an apartment in Hoover, and Al's wife scored a sales job at the Riverchase Galleria mall.

Mike Heathcott, who shares a place with one of the interns in the Barons' office, isn't much for small talk this morning. The twenty-four-year-old right-hander has a reddish scar on his pitching shoulder from off-season surgery and has been describing some mysterious back pain to Vern.

They're all dull on the subject of Michael. Of course they're preoccupied right now, but you also sense that while having Michael around is somewhat interesting for them, what's there to say? He's Michael and he's there. They're acquainted with him but they don't really know him. He's one of the guys but of course he *isn't*: he plays Yahtzee and dominoes and cards with them on bus rides, and Ping-Pong in the clubhouse, but *he's* the only one who needs a police escort out of the stadium after games; he's the one who gets mobbed everywhere; he's the one who'll pop up on a TV commercial while they're killing time at the Ramada; he's the one whose lost jewelry nearly brings a game to a halt.

Yes, he's Michael Jordan, American idol, but these guys are human beings, and to Al Levine the most trifling matter in Al Levine's life is more important than anything. Right now Al's pushing for a promotion up the White Sox chain, Mike Heathcott's trying to come back from surgery, Rogelio Nunez is struggling with Double-A pitching, and none are much interested in talking about Michael Jordan.

While Mike and then Al throw to Nunie—wearing only shorts and sneakers, with Ping-Pong-sized balls attached to their ankles, knees, hips, elbows, and shoulders for a computerized analysis of their mechanics—I chat with Lanier Johnson, ASMI's vice president of public relations.

ASMI is the research arm of HealthSouth, a publicly traded rehab corporation whose doctors treat afflicted Barons, and the connection has made neighbors of Michael and Mr. Johnson in the Greystone section of Hoover. "Yes," Johnson says in an amiable drawl, "as part of our Southern hospitality, HealthSouth is providing a house it owns for Michael to live in while he's here. It's in Greystone, where I live myself, one of the nicer areas in Hoover—a gated community, relatively new, with a wonderful golf course. Michael is a member of the Greystone Country Club. It's a positive public-relations gesture, since Michael coming to Birmingham is such a big event."

The ASMI house had been up for sale, Johnson says, but was taken off the market for Michael. It will go up for sale again when he leaves. Meanwhile, it's enough to accommodate Michael and his wife and three children, who will reportedly be joining him at the end of the Chicago school year.

Johnson says his friend Johnny Walker, the president of

Meeting Mister Falk

Crown Mercedes in Birmingham, set Michael up with wheels for the summer. "Obviously it's beneficial to have Michael Jordan riding around in a Mercedes with the Crown logo on the back."

So much for the skeptics who say Michael won't tolerate the minor-league grind for long.

Johnson thinks Michael is wonderful. He met him at the country club last week and played in his foursome in a pro-am tournament earlier this week.

"From the first tee all the way through, about three and a half hours, his disposition was just *out*-standin'. We had a big crowd out there to see Michael and the tour players, and no ropes or gallery control, but Michael was very congenial, very polite. He'd have to caution 'em once in a while—'Look out, kids, I've got spikes on and I don't wanna step on anybody so y'all watch out'—all the while signin' autographs and standin' for pictures to be made. All of our group was very impressed."

He seems impressed that Michael wasn't rude. It's the mentality that not only ignores the fact that Michael can't afford to be rude but assumes that celebrities somehow *should* be, that they've earned the right to be, and that we should give them high marks for not availing themselves of that right; that we should applaud them for merely being civil, which is the *least* we expect from each other.

———

Now that Pika has seemingly granted me entry in Birmingham, I decide to skip the last two games of this home stand and head for Florida, where the Barons play six games next week.

I stay off the interstates to catch as much as I can of the real world. In threadbare black communities down through Alabama I feel like I'm way back in time—fifty years, eighty, who knows? At an intersection in some faceless burg I pull up alongside two middle-aged men in an old pickup, working stiffs whose annual pay for some kind of backbreaking work probably doesn't amount to what HealthSouth's hospitality is saving Michael in rent this summer. I'm reminded of something Michael once said about the ironies of life: "[In restaurants] they want to buy me dinner. But I don't need it. The person who needs a free meal can't get it. The rich get richer. If that doesn't show you how everything is backwards in society, nothing will."

Down past Dothan, Alabama, on the two-lane road, the occasional crossroads are identified by number only, like South County Road 75. Out in front of a run-down gas station sits a rusted-out school bus with "Mt. Carmel Church" handpainted on the side and the hood propped open. I'm pretty sure it's been in that same spot, hood propped open, for weeks or months or longer.

By the time I pass through Climax, Florida in the early evening and hit the Tallahassee Highway in Bainbridge, things start looking tropical. Both sides of the country road are lined by tall trees with skinny trunks and only a little vegetation at the very top. I start seeing weird, gnarly, Van Goghesque trees—Spanish moss hanging creepily from the branches—that seem to have lives of their own. Southern Gothic.

I start seeing palm trees in Havana. Down past Tallahassee I breeze through hamlets and less-than-hamlets, some comprising not much more than a weedy, faded, old-fashioned motor court advertising "Cheap Rates"; a one-pump gas station and market; and an incongruously new Subway sandwich shop. (Subway is everywhere.) In the stretches in between, roadside stands with handpainted and frequently misspelled

Meeting Mister Falk

signs offer "Boiled Peanuts," "Paper-Shell Peanuts," "P-Nut Brittle," "Sweet Vidalia Onions," and "Fresh-Shelled Pecans, $1.99/pd."

It's quiet, slow, peaceful, but the sight of a roadside rest area in the deepening dusk reminds me I'm in Florida, where horrors lurk beneath the most serene surface. One of the big stories last summer was the wave of murders at Florida rest areas. Just last week I read about more craziness down here—a Swedish tourist strangled in a sandy field over in Palm Beach County.

So it's calm, as I cruise, in an ominous Southern-Gothic way—like the quiet, seemingly tranquil bayou, where the dangers lie hidden below the surface before materializing suddenly and brutally.

On Sunday, the Chicago Bulls blow a fourth-quarter lead to go down 0–1 to the hated Knicks in the Eastern Conference semifinals. Monday, a certain erstwhile Knickslayer plays his first baseball game in Orlando.

Before going to the park, I call Falk as requested.

"Falk Enterprises," the secretary up in Washington, D.C. answers, and asks who I'd like to speak to. David Falk, I say, and she says she'll put me through to Mr. Falk's office.

Another secretary picks up; I ask *her* for Falk. She asks my business with "Mr. Falk," referring to the money-man in a tone usually reserved for "Mr. President." I tell her I don't know: I'm writing a book about Michael Jordan and I've had some contact with Barbara Allen and I got a message to please call Falk so I'm calling, that's all.

She puts me on hold—then comes on *again*, for no reason but to inform me, "Mr. Falk will speak to you now."

Just put him on, lady! I'm impressed, OK?

ROOKIE

When "Mister" Falk at last comes on the line, I identify myself and tell him I got a message from Chris Pika to call him; I don't know why.

I'm startled when Mister Falk says *he* doesn't know anything about it either. He says *he* got a message from Pika saying I was going to call him because I was upset about the way the Barons were treating me.

Huh?

But hey, I'm willing to talk. I tell Mister Falk I *have* been unhappy with the Barons, it's true, but I expect things to work out now that I've gotten Michael's OK.

At which point Mister Falk, in his icy money-man way, lets me know it's *not* OK. "You're trying to make money off Michael Jordan and you're not sharing the proceeds with Michael Jordan charities . . . "

He leaves it hanging. It's my chance to make an offer. But I'm speechless, stunned by the brass of this notorious ten-percenter accusing *me* of trying to make money off Michael Jordan. My head fills with Falklore. An NBA general manager calling him "the agent from hell." Michael himself once saying, "I probably wouldn't like him if he wasn't with me. He's the Rick Mahorn of agents." The owlish, pasty Mister Falk letting on that he sees himself as more a Don Corleone type: "If you're powerful, if you have the ultimate clout, you don't have to yell and scream. You could quietly [make your request] . . . and the guy would say, 'OK, you're the Godfather, here it is'—and you'd walk out."

Still flabbergasted, I can't manage more than a wimpy, "I'm supposed to . . . contribute to Michael's charities?"

"Or," Mister Falk says casually, "Michael might just want to give the money to his children."

I stammer around some more. "Ummm . . . Barbara Allen

told me she thought it would be OK with Michael if I'm around as long as I'm not asking for interviews for a biography. And Michael told me OK."

No. Because they knew nothing of my project, and because Michael has an arrangement with the publisher of *Rare Air* and *I Can't Accept Not Trying*, Michael will not be available to me at all. No hard feelings, it's just that it's Mister Falk's job to look out for Michael.

But, I protest, I told Michael himself that I don't need private interviews to write my book, I just want locker-room access, and he said OK. Besides, the team is supposed to give me access anyway.

"*No.* You're trying to make money off Michael's name and accomplishments."

"*And,*" I interject, "off my labors and my humble gifts."

But Mister Falk's ready for me. "*No,*" he repeats, and muses, "Who knows? Michael might want to write his own diary of the season."

In any case, Mister Falk asserts once more that I'll be getting no cooperation. Every inch a gentleman, however, he wishes me luck on my book before signing off.

The Magic Bus

*"Pretending is a virtue. If you can't pretend,
you can't be king."*

— Luigi Pirandello, *Liolà*

Monday is a big day in Orlando, home of Sea World and
Disney World and Epcot Center and soon, according to billboards, a new Planet Hollywood restaurant. Michael's here!
Yesterday's *Sentinel* had a long piece on "the business of Jordan," talking about all the extra income for the Barons and all
Southern League clubs from ticket sales and concessions and
so forth. Today's paper—front page, sports page, all over—is
full of Michael.

At 4 P.M., three hours before the game, there's a buzz around
old Tinker Field: cars pulling in, cops, parking attendants, TV
crews, kids waiting for the gates to open. A cop says some of
these people have been here for three hours already. I pick up
my press pass at the will-call window and breeze in. No problem here: I called the Orlando Cubs last week, my editor faxed
them that I'm legit, and they let me know my pass would be
waiting. The way it usually works.

Tinker Field was built in 1914 and later renamed for Joe
Tinker (of Tinker-to-Evers-to-Chance fame), who managed
Orlando's Florida State League team in the 1920s and later
made Orlando his retirement home. Today the ballpark stands

The Magic Bus

literally in the shadow of the Citrus Bowl; the backside of the football bleachers looms up behind the right-field fence and runs along it out to dead center.

TV crews are setting up down on the field, on top of the dugouts, everywhere. Reporters mill around on the field— thirty-five reporters from a hundred miles around are expected tonight, as opposed to the usual three locals. A chatty young woman from the *Florida Times-Union* in Jacksonville, the Barons' next stop, has come over to watch these three games and write a couple of pieces on Michaelmania.

The early crowd surrounds a batting cage behind the first-base stands. Obviously Michael is taking some licks, and I'm headed over that way with the chatty lady from Jacksonville when we encounter a high-energy fellow in an Orlando Cubs cap who turns out to be Connie Cowal, the forty-two-year-old director of minor-league operations for the Chicago Cubs. He's charged up. He says he's been pointing to tonight since the January day when the White Sox invited Michael to spring training and it became conceivable that he would make this trip with the Barons.

At the sight of our tape recorders, Cowal shifts into over-drive. "It's great. This whole thing is great not only for the Southern League and all its cities and teams . . . not only for Orlando, where the Orlando Cubs have been gaining in popularity and fan base ever since we became the Orlando Cubs two years ago. There are a lot of pluses in this thing, and it all revolves around a terrific superstar and a great gentleman in Michael Jordan.

"Look at all the kids, the families. I've seen lots of dads with their sons, pointing out who this great person is. You know, when Michael said he wanted to fulfill a boyhood dream by playing baseball, I think a lot of kids probably said, 'Michael

ROOKIE

Jordan likes baseball? Mom, Dad, get me a bat, a ball, a glove—I wanna be like Mike.' I think baseball needed that. Baseball needs heroes. This is just a wondrous thing for the sport."

Then, from the general wondrousness to the benefits for the Orlando Cubs: "This is another one of a lot of great things to happen down here since the Tribune Company bought the club. We had Mike Harkey pitch down here. We had Ryne Sandberg rehabilitate and play a couple of games here last year. Frank Castillo pitched here two weeks ago. And tonight Jose Guzman, the Chicago Cubs' number two big-league pitcher, is here on rehab. This is just another step for us, and for the fans too . . . so they can identify with the Orlando Cubs and say, 'Wow, this is hot, this is great.'

"Look at these Orlando Cubs hats we're giving away to-night. It's Giveaway Hat Night. Normally you'd say that if you've got Michael Jordan you don't need to give anything away, but this is showtime for us. We want fans to say, 'And I get a *hat*?' We're playing Birmingham in these three games, and they happen to have a promising guy named Michael Jordan with them, but we are marketing the Orlando Cubs."

Attendance here, Cowal says, usually depends on the promotion. "A Hat Night is a big deal—you might have three, four, five thousand people." With their "growing fan base," the Cubs are averaging 2,247 at home so far.

"We sold out the reserve and box seats to these three games in just a couple of days. Last week we announced a sellout for tonight on the basis of general-admission sales. We'll have a crowd of around six thousand, which is what Tinker Field comfortably holds. We could have sold eight, ten, twelve thousand tickets with extra bleachers and standing room, but we tried to stay within our limits. We're here every night, all summer, and we want it to be comfortable and enjoyable for those who come tonight so they'll come back."

We're interrupted by the slow wave of humanity coming our way, threatening to sweep us under: the mob surrounding Michael as he makes his way from the batting cage to the field. In the middle of the pack you can see his dark bald head above the rest. He's surrounded by four burly cops and the ever-present Pika, with reporters and photographers clamoring around them and dozens of kids and curious adults forming the clamorous knot around *them*.

It's as if he's some exotic creature in a cage formed by Pika and the cops, with people gawking and trying to reach through the bars and touch him. They scream his name, thrust out things for him to sign, snap his picture. Michael just moves along as if he doesn't notice, eyes straight ahead and slightly downcast, unseeing, in what celebrities call "blindsight"—not acknowledging anyone, not acknowledging that any of it is even happening. Can't afford to. Can't stop, can't look around. Can't be human.

He escapes the crush only when it reaches the gate by the first-base dugout and security personnel keep out all but Michael and his phalanx and we of the legitimate media. Michael crosses to the Barons' third-base dugout and vanishes into the tunnel to the clubhouse.

Writers, photographers, batboys, and stray others hang out around the dugout. On top of it, a spiffy local TV reporter is doing his "stand-up" for the evening news. He gives his high-octane spiel; then the cameraman pans around at the kids lined up along the railings hoping for a close look at Michael. A crew from another station is doing the same thing in foul territory down the left-field side.

Out in front of the dugout, the glib radio man Curt Bloom,

ROOKIE

"C.B.," wearing sneakers and shorts and a damp Barons T-shirt, thumbs the sweat off his forehead. C.B. likes feeling part of things (wants to learn golf "because everyone in this business plays golf") and he's been out shagging flies during Barons batting practice.

C.B. loves his gig. "I'll tell you what, you never catch up on your sleep in this business," he sighs after describing the nine-and-a-half-hour bus trip down here after Saturday night's game—but quickly adds, as if he's just blasphemed, "I can't complain, though. I'm doing what I wanted to do all my life.

"How did I get this job? I started in baseball when I was twenty-four, but it took me three years to get into the minor leagues. I was disc-jockeying at an adult-contemporary radio station and meanwhile sending out tapes and going to the winter-league meetings, where everyone in baseball gets together and just schmoozes—you talk *industry*, you meet the general managers. That's how it all began. I was fortunate enough in 1988 that the GM of the Bakersfield Dodgers said, 'Hey, come on out to California, do a little broadcasting and some other things.' And you go from there. Every year you make up your resumé and your tape and send it out.

"You've got to be willing to pack your bags. In one calendar year I had three addresses: Woodbridge, Virginia [home of the White Sox organization's Single-A club, the Prince William Cannons]; Huntsville, Alabama; and Birmingham, Alabama. But I knew that's what it takes."

It also takes a willingness to put on a tie and jacket and sell advertising in the off-season. "Radio ads, program ads, outfield signs, promotions—if it exists in a ballpark, we sell it. If it doesn't, we'll invent it and sell it. Everyone in our office, from Bill Hardekopf on down . . . from October through March, we

The Magic Bus

all look the same, dress the same, act the same. We have our meetings, we coordinate, and we go out and sell."

It's what C.B. has to do in order to spend summers as voice of the Barons, which he hopes will earn him a ticket to the big leagues. "But I'll tell ya," he adds, waving an arm to take in the advertising around Tinker Field, "when you personally make a sale—and this is the God's honest truth—it's one of the ultimate highs, it really is."

All around us, reporters interview Michael's youthful teammates, the coaches, Terry Francona. Even the driver of the famous bus, a tall greying man named Dale Richardson, is surrounded by a half-dozen scribes taking down his every word.

Michael's teammates might seem like grown men from the distance of the press box or even the stands, but up close they're revealed as the post-adolescents they are by their looks and their banter. They would just as soon not be bothered by reporters—not to talk about someone besides themselves— and they're predictably bland on the subject of Michael.

I find Randy Hood, the outfielder who told Tom Brokaw for an NBC *Now* feature, "I resent [Michael joining the club] in a way because this is all I've worked for my whole life and a guy can come right in and get the opportunity I've been looking for." The poor guy gets trembly at the mention of that gaffe and says, "They kind of misquoted me, took it out of context. They kind of made me out to be the bad guy." He's backing away as if I'm carrying the plague. "I really don't have anything else to say . . . "

"Did anyone else feel that way?"

"Not that I've noticed. I really don't have anything—"

I butt in, "Has it been fun having him around?" Quick, give him a chance to sing Michael's praises if he wants.

ROOKIE

—but Hood is retreating down the dugout steps: "I really don't have anything else to say."

I don't see Barry Johnson, the pitcher who told Brokaw, "I think it's a case of a guy who's got some connections and a big name taking advantage of it." The others sound like shortstop Glenn DiSarcina (brother of California Angels infielder Gary), who says, "He's a good guy and I think he's gone out of his way to try and fit in." Scott Tedder, the former basketball star, says, "Going to the White House, visiting with President Reagan, being the first Division III team to be in the Oval Office was the highlight of my life. Now, playing with Michael Jordan is just icing on the cake.

"Just to see the way he handles the media," Tedder adds, "the way he stays in control of a situation and always knows what to say . . . I think everybody in the clubhouse can learn from him."

Tedder clearly *has* learned how to play it safety-first with the media. Randy Hood didn't learn it in time.

When Michael reappears, he doesn't linger to be photographed or interviewed but skips up the dugout steps past center fielder Kerry Valrie, who's talking to reporters, and joshes, "Hey, you gonna throw or what? Or you gonna do a press conference?" Valrie follows. Out in left field, they throw.

I approach the smiling, round-faced, thirty-five-year-old batting coach, Mike Barnett, in the grass behind the plate. "Barney," who's in his fifth year in the White Sox organization, never played pro ball and is something of a featured character for the first time in his life. If Michael makes progress, baseball people will know Mike Barnett.

After plugging a fresh chew in his lower lip, Barnett tells me that his reaction when he heard Michael was taking up baseball was unlike many purists'. "I said, 'Great.' I wasn't going to

The Magic Bus

make any judgments until I saw him. Anybody who's that great an athlete and has the kind of work ethic he seemed to have, why *couldn't* he make it? And I thought it was great when he came to our team. He's a great guy to be around. If you saw what he has to go through every day, it's not easy, but he's a pro, not only in the athletic sense but in how he handles himself as a person."

We talk a little hitting. When I remark that Michael seems to have altered his stance lately, laying the bat flat on his shoulder as he awaits the pitch, Barnett says, "It gets him in position by cutting out one move. He was starting with his hands up high and bringing 'em down, and now we've just eliminated that move so he doesn't have to start his swing so soon.

"He made the adjustment very easily, which is a credit to him. This is what I've seen in good hitters over the years: they always go on feel. The first night I said, 'Try your hands here and see how it feels,' he went 0-for-4. Later I asked him how it felt and I was expecting, like, 'Aw, I don't know,' but he didn't confuse the results with how it felt. He said, 'It felt great, I really felt comfortable,' and he's carried on with it, and he's making adjustments daily."

Does Barnett foresee a day when Michael can contend with major-league pitching?

He hedges. "Well, you aren't going to see a lot better stuff in the big leagues than in Double A. Your Madduxes and Clemenses stick out, but the everyday pitchers are pretty much the same guys as you see here; they just have a little better control, more consistency. More command."

Another reporter joins us and asks Barnett about Michael's lack of power: no homers, no triples, only two doubles in nineteen games. Barnett serenely expels a stream of juice and

ROOKIE

readjusts his chew. "He hasn't hit a homer in a game yet, but in spring training he wasn't even hitting them out in batting practice. Now he's hitting 'em in BP, and I mean not just clearing the fence—he's *crushin'* 'em. So that's progress. But that's nothing we're even concerned about. If he was a slow runner, you'd say, 'He's gotta hit the ball out of the park,' but he's got eight or nine stolen bases [among Southern League leaders]. So if the power does start coming in game situations like it's coming in BP, you're looking at a guy with some tremendous tools."

We'll see. I haven't noticed Michael crushin' 'em in BP, but maybe I've been there on the wrong days.

Before they chase the press off the field, I introduce myself to Terry Francona. "I'm writing a book about Michael's summer in the minor leagues. I'd like to spend some time with you and hear about your experience with Michael, your life as a minor-league manager, everything."

Francona's friendly, but he's hustling off to the clubhouse. "Shouldn't be a problem. We play mostly at night, so I've got time during the day. Get in touch with me up in Birmingham and we can set something up."

Things are coming together.

———

The muggiest weather I've experienced in Alabama doesn't begin to compare with this. Open your mouth and a puff of saunalike air hits the back of your throat, briefly taking your breath away. I hope to escape in the press box but it turns out to be a small, open-air affair, as antiquated as the rest of Tinker Field. No escape.

They're serving soft drinks and spicy chicken wings. Cubs staff have laid out stacks of game notes and all sorts of printed

The Magic Bus

trivia that I suspect isn't part of the everyday spread. You certainly can't miss the all-caps memo regarding the press conference Michael holds after his first game in each town, which is the only press access he permits on the road:

> MICHAEL JORDAN WILL HOST A POST-GAME PRESS CON-FERENCE TONIGHT ONLY. THE CONFERENCE WILL BEGIN 25 MINUTES FOLLOWING TONIGHT'S GAME. PLEASE WAIT 15 MINUTES BEFORE SETTING UP DOWN ON THE FIELD. ALSO, PLEASE LIMIT YOUR QUESTIONS TO BASEBALL ONLY.

The quaint old park is overflowing by game time. The tops of the dugouts are covered with photographers and TV cameras plus some Cubs sponsors and local wheels kicked back in lounge chairs. Several dozen people are sitting in folding chairs on top of some aluminum trailers behind the right-field fence, at the base of the towering Citrus Bowl. (The trailers turn out to be offices for the staff preparing for World Cup soccer in July.) The press box is overflowing, too: I and a bunch of others wind up sitting down below in a roped-off row of the bleachers.

After the ceremonial first pitches are thrown by local TV personality Buckaroo Bob and the manager of a local Steak 'n Shake, a Cubs sponsor, the Cubs are introduced and take their positions one by one, Little Leaguers bolting out behind them as in Birmingham. After the anthem, the Little Leaguers run off the field and the hum of anticipation begins as Jose Guzman starts his warm-up tosses and Michael, recently moved from seventh to second in the Barons' lineup, comes out of the dugout into the on-deck circle. The hum becomes a roar when leadoff man Doug Brady goes down and Michael steps in to face Guzman, the rehabbing big-leaguer (78–72 lifetime, 12–10 last season).

ROOKIE

Guzman promptly freezes Michael with two big-league breaking pitches: strike one, strike two. But when he tries to sneak a fastball past him, Michael cracks one deep to right center that the right-fielder hauls down only after a long run. An out, but good work against a major leaguer who doesn't look too far from top shape. The crowd keeps roaring as Michael jogs back to the dugout.

They roar again a couple minutes later when the Barons are retired and he jogs out to right field. They can't believe they're seeing him.

The between-inning promotions start early with the Ice Cream Toss: hit the target with a ball, win a cone at a local parlor; miss, and they tell you to move up closer. There are no losers.

A half inning later, a guy wins a $10 gift certificate at Goodling's Supermarket by making contact with two out of three Wiffle Ball pitches. Big ball, hard to miss.

For a while it's as low-key as any other minor-league game. The outs and innings accumulate as people eat, chat, wander around, take babies to the bathroom. It doesn't matter who wins. It's a night at the ballpark, that's all.

But when Michael strides out of the dugout with his black bat for the second time, I'm reminded of those old TV commercials—"When E. F. Hutton talks, people listen"—in which entire crowds go silent and strain to hear when a Hutton man starts talking stocks. The instant Michael appears, people hurry back to their seats, put conversations on hold, put the bottle in baby's mouth and tell the kids, "Watch, now! There he is!" You can feel all the diffuse energy in the park suddenly focussed *there*, all eyes riveted on the tall, lanky figure in the on-deck circle. Then, after the cheer that accompanies him up to the plate, a hush covers the place.

The Magic Bus

This time, Michael goes after Guzman's first pitch and tops a bouncer to the third baseman, who easily pegs him out.

And the fans go back to chatting, reading, eating, wandering around, their attention refocussing only for the more amusing promotions. In the Dizzy Bat Race, that Southern League staple, a guy in his twenties survives his girlfriend, comically, to win a TGI Friday's gift certificate. A couple of old duffers win dinners at Jackson Hole Steak House by sinking putts into a container that a blind man couldn't miss.

In the sixth inning, with Guzman out of the game, Michael draws a walk and steals second. When he's left stranded at inning's end, the eleven-year-old midget batboy trots out and gazes up adoringly as Michael, waiting for a teammate to bring out his cap and mitt, removes his helmet and batting gloves. Michael notices, and as he hands over his gear he says something and reaches down to give the kid a chuck on the shoulder. The kid trots back to his post looking like he's been crowned king.

Michael fouls out in the seventh inning, after which about a third of the crowd of 6,422—the largest of the season here, by far—streams out of Tinker Field.

As if Michael is going to do an autograph session for several thousand after the game, the ones who stay are the kids wearing caps and holding balls and gloves and programs, tended by their parents. As soon as the Barons retire the last Cub in the bottom of the ninth and trot in to slap high fives around the mound, these faithful clamor down as close as they can to the dugout—the kids holding objects to be signed, parents poised behind them with cameras.

Even after both teams disappear through their dugouts, they wait. They must know Michael is coming back for his press conference.

ROOKIE

A table with a chair behind it and a microphone on top is set up outside the third-base line, and after the fifteen minutes specified in the press-box memo we all shuffle down to the field. The TV crews arrange themselves in front of the table where Michael will preside, and everyone else fans out from there, thirty or forty people in all: local radio jocks with tape recorders and mikes, reporters from all over Florida with notebooks. I'm wondering why in the world I wore long pants in suffocating weather like this. A writer from the *Orlando Business Journal* says, "It's nights like this in early May that convince me we'll never get a major-league team here or in St. Petersburg."

Pika circulates, now checking the mike on the table, now reminding people to restrict their questions to baseball, now telling a photographer he'll have to back up a little more, a little more, a little more.

Presently Jose Guzman, dressed in slacks and a flowered short-sleeve shirt, his dark curly hair still wet from the shower, comes out through the Orlando dugout. He's been asked to share his thoughts on Michael. A few of us walk over to record them.

"He heet the ball pretty good the first time," says Guzman, not wholly comfortable with English. "He took a couple of breakeen' balls; then I tried to go up and away but he reached it. That tells you that when you have a tall guy with long arms, you gotta throw inside."

Someone asks, "Any extra pressure, facing Jordan?"

Guzman, a major leaguer, smiles. "Well, I didn't want to go back to Chicago and have the guys say, 'What happened with Michael Jordan? He got a hit off you.' "

A minute later Guzman is gone and Michael at last appears out of the third-base dugout, accompanied by Pika, naturally,

The Magic Bus

and a few cops and Cubs personnel. The kids still waiting behind the dugout whoop it up.

Though it's 10 P.M., things are unnaturally bright under the big lights as Michael strolls across the grass and sits down behind the table. He's wearing creamy linen slacks and a matching sleeveless vest over a black T-shirt (a *classy* T-shirt), with thin creamy socks and shiny, wafer-thin black loafers. A black motorman's cap perches on the famous pate. He's got a diamond stud in his left ear, a big gold-and-diamond wedding ring on his huge left hand, and around his neck a heavy gold chain with diamonds, presumably the one he lost for a couple of innings the other night.

As usual, Michael is bland and correct. "It's been a learning experience every day. I think I played pretty good defense today and was able to steal a base or two. I just tried to contribute in any way I could. There's gonna be days you don't get any hits, but when the team wins, that's all you can ask for. I just gotta keep working at it."

Is his motivation still strong? "Oh yeah. I'm very happy with what I'm doing. I've got a long way to go, but every day I take something away, even though I might not get any hits. Like, I faced a major-league pitcher tonight, got a look at some of the stuff he was throwing, and I was able to stay in there and make contact. It was a good test for all of us, a measuring stick: see how well you can do against a major-league pitcher."

How does he fit in here, given the age difference between him and his teammates, and, more importantly, given who he is?

"It varies. I feel older than these guys in a sense, like their big brother, and I try to tell 'em what's right and wrong in certain situations, like dealing with the press. In other ways I feel like their *little* brother: they're teaching me to play the game of baseball. In terms of who I hang out with, I hang out with everybody. Mostly the coaches," he adds with a smile, "because they're closer to my age.

"But I've always been able to fluctuate from older people to younger people. I don't think there's a generation gap. I respect them as people and certainly as players. I think they do the same to me. Maybe a little bit more from them to me than from me to them. But I understand that. I think a lot of my accolades from basketball preceded me to this situation to where they give me a lot more respect than I'm asking. I just want to be their friend and be part of the team."

Someone blurts out, "Did the Bulls' loss yesterday disappoint you?"

Pika—who's been playing the power broker, hovering near Michael and pointing at whichever reporter he'll permit to ask the next question—instantly steps out, waving his arms. "Gentlemen, gentlemen, let's keep it to baseball," he insists—only to back off, abashed, when Michael simply shrugs and says, "I kinda knew basketball questions were coming," and then addresses the questioner. "I felt they had a good opportunity to beat New York; New York probably took 'em for granted. This Bulls team isn't as bad as people think, even though I'm not playing. I'd probably help them a little bit," he allows modestly, "but they're still a good team."

Before another question is posed, Pika steps in reminding us to stick to baseball, but when someone promptly shouts something about Horace Grant, he seems to realize no one's paying any attention to him and Michael isn't going to back him up.

Michael says Grant and the Bulls need to quit talking about what would happen if he were still with them. "When I was there we had big leads and lost 'em sometimes. They're talking 'if,' and we don't wanna live in 'if' territory. They did a good

The Magic Bus

job without me all season long and never said 'if,' so don't start saying 'if' now. They're very capable of winning; they just gotta believe in themselves."

Someone wants to know how Michael is adjusting to the unromantic reality of minor-league baseball, particularly the everyday schedule.

"It's exactly what I thought it would be. Baseball is a crash course for me. For me to get better rapidly I have to play every day and see all the different situations as soon as possible. Life in the minors? People have made it out to be so bad, but it *isn't* so bad. The game is very humbling but I'm happy to be here. I don't think I'm ever too big to live like a normal person."

Michael's a little out of touch with normalcy by now. Minor-league life isn't cushy for anyone but him. The players earn about $1,000 a month (for seven months only), and all except Michael have to pay rent, pay for transportation, pay to play golf if they want to play golf. They share cheesy apartments, sometimes with two or three roommates, and eat at Wendy's and McDonald's and Pizza Hut except for the occasional splurge at a TGI Friday's on the road, where they receive a $16-a-day meal allowance. They drive used cars, or *share* used cars. If they're married, their wives get jobs at the mall. If they can.

Asked if he thinks his critics are surprised by his play so far, Michael says, "I think it shows them not to prejudge people. To this point I think I've put a 'maybe' into their quotes instead of a 'not.' And that's a big step, but it's not the ultimate. The ultimate is to take that 'maybe' out and make it a 'yes'—'Yes, he can play this game.' "

Has he heard from other players, major leaguers? Spring-training reports said a lot of real ballplayers resented him for trying out.

ROOKIE

"A lot of past and present players have issued support," Michael says. "Deion [Sanders] wanted to come down and teach me how to steal bases. George Brett called. Frank Thomas, Dave Justice, a lot of people have called and issued support for what I'm trying to do. They don't see it as degrading to the game because they've seen my work ethic and seen that I don't think I can just walk onto the field and accomplish what they've accomplished over a lifetime. If anything, I've showed the normal person . . ."

Uh-oh.

". . . that if you work hard you can achieve whatever you want. Not just in baseball, but in whatever you feel you're capable of doing. I think a lot of people miss that point. So many people are envious of what I'm doing, they miss the point that the motivational factor of what I'm doing can be passed on . . . not just to kids, but to people who are having troubled times. That's what keeps me going forward, no matter what negative comments I get.

"You should never give up on what you believe in," Michael sums up. "If I really didn't believe in what I'm doing and was just out here for the media attention, the criticism would be correct, but that's not why I'm here. It just so happens that you guys pay attention to what I'm doing."

"All right, gentlemen," Pika interjects at this point, stepping in and waving his arms like a football referee signaling that the play is dead. And Michael, after posing for a picture with Orlando's little batboy, disappears into the dugout (Pika right behind) and on through to the clubhouse and then out.

His teammates await him aboard the Jordancruiser.

———

The next morning's *Tampa Tribune* reveals that Michael did

not, after all, lay out $350,000 for the fancy new bus. A Barons' spokesperson would only say that there was "an arrangement" between "Jordan, his agent and the club."

No, I'm not surprised Mister Falk is involved. No, I'm not surprised that, though it's not true, millions of people around the world believe Michael Jordan bought his teammates a new luxury bus out of the goodness of his heart.

"Yes, I talked to [Mister Falk] many times," I'm eventually told by Jim Thrasher of Thrasher Brothers Tours, a "regional charter carrier" which has provided the Barons' transportation for thirteen years.

The truth's not as good a story as Michael plunking down $350,000 to treat his teammates to a new luxury bus. In the first place, the Barons don't own a bus but *lease* one every season, paying Thrasher Brothers to provide a bus and driver to carry them about 18,000 miles in the course of six months. The updated, refurbished MC-9 the Barons were using is a *very* nice bus itself, Jim Thrasher says, but by the time Michael arrived in Birmingham, Mister Falk had arranged for Michael to meet with Thrasher about a better one.

"I spent an hour with Michael. He was very pleasant. He said he wanted a new bus, a forty-five-footer, with a lounge and enough room for him to stretch out. He admitted he didn't know much about buses, but that was what he wanted. MCI [Motor Coach Industry, builder of the MC-9 the Barons were using] had already called after they heard Michael might be interested in a new bus, but I called all three major manufacturers. All three FedExed me their proposals, knowing the kind of publicity they would get if Michael Jordan was riding their bus. MCI had the best bus, their MC-11. They had a coach in Atlanta that didn't have a lounge in back; they brought down a lounge from a bus in Chicago, and within a week of the

ROOKIE

order we had the new bus in Birmingham, in time for the first trip to Chattanooga."

So if the Barons don't own the bus, Michael at least paid the higher lease rate, right?

Wrong. "Because of the deal Thrasher Brothers got from MCI, and because of the nice publicity we got because Michael was riding the bus, our rates didn't change at all for the Barons," says Jim Thrasher. Thrasher notes that he's been interviewed by *NBC Nightly News* and *Hard Copy*, and has appeared on drive-time radio shows from Atlanta to Seattle; even a London station called. "It ended up being a deal that worked out very well for everyone: Thrasher Brothers, which is known all over the United States now, the Birmingham Barons, Michael Jordan, and MCI, the company that built the bus."

How about the story that Michael shelled out $350,000 to buy the bus?

"We never counteracted the story that Michael bought it— we were so busy, so much going on . . . "

I wonder when Michael's going to fess up.

———

Michael winds up the three-game series 2-for-12, including a sharp double down the left-field line, and leaves town with a .250 batting average.

The Orlando Cubs draw 19,523 paying customers over the three nights, only 6,000 less than their total for twelve previous dates. General manager Roger Wexelberg says the club hopes they impressed the people of Orlando and made some new fans.

Believe It or Not

*"Fame has also this great drawback, that if we pursue
it we must direct our lives in such a way as to please the
fancy of men, avoiding what they dislike and seeking
what is pleasing to them."*

— Spinoza, *Correction of the Understanding*

Florida's got the muggiest weather in the country, the longest
stoplights, the most senior citizens, and countless tourists driving RVs or towing boats behind their cars. The combination
makes driving miserable for hand-to-mouth *artistes* who can't
afford air-conditioning in their little tin ovens.

South of Jacksonville I stop in St. Augustine, which was
settled by Europeans forty years before Jamestown and is one
of several Florida communities claiming the title of "Nation's
Oldest City." It's hot, bright, and dusty on the streets in the old
Spanish quarter, not much activity except for slow-moving
tourists and a few horse-drawn surreys for hire, driven by
wizened black men on the streets between Ponce de Leon's
reputed Fountain of Youth and Potter's Wax Museum and the
St. Augustine Alligator Farm.

I tour the Ripley's Believe It or Not! Museum and shake my
head at seeing the Lord's Prayer written on a grain of rice; the
Skeleton Dude, five-foot-seven and forty-eight pounds; Robert Wadlow, eight-foot-eleven with size 37AAA shoes; the
Human Unicorn with a thirteen-inch horn growing out of the

back of his head; the seventeen-inch-tall dwarf from ancient Alexandria, imprisoned (for treason) in a parrot's cage; the two-headed calf; the three-legged stallion; the four-eyed kitten; and Beauregard, the six-legged steer.

Yet as I head on up Route A1A to Jacksonville, not far from the Atlantic Ocean, and my thoughts inevitably circle back to Michael's world, those wonders seem trifling beside the colossal self-importance, the breathtaking arrogance, and the believe-it-or-not greed I've recently encountered.

In Jacksonville, the *Florida Times-Union* trumpets Michael's arrival in nearly every section. The front-page Michaelmania piece says the Jacksonville Suns, averaging 3,100 fans at home, expect to fit 10,000 into 8,200-seat Wolfson Park for each of these three games, including roped-off standing-room areas. The club has ordered more than a ton of hot dogs, four times the typical order. It's said that Mickey Mantle and ex–big leaguers Hank Bauer, "Moose" Skowron, and Cal McLish, vacationing nearby, are coming.

The lifestyle section features a color picture of the Jordancruiser, and a sidebar to the accompanying story makes a bus-to-bus comparison: the Barons' new ride costs $350,000 versus Jacksonville's $60,000 1983 model, boasts six TVs to Jacksonville's four, and so on. Such a bus! *NBC Nightly News* did a story on it last week. Pika (quoted in the papers wherever the Barons go) says he's gotten hundreds of requests from reporters wanting to ride the bus. Jim Thrasher of Thrasher Brothers Tours says he's talked to over 150 reporters.

Outfielder Scott Tedder, asked where Michael sits on the bus, says, "Anywhere he wants. It's his bus."

The sports section, of course, is bursting with Jordan plus all the details about tonight's starting times, ticket prices, you name it. A big headline, "AIR of Confidence"; a big color

Believe It or Not

picture; a long piece that goes on to cover most of page seven. A column by an older guy reminiscing about famous players who've appeared in Jacksonville—Babe Ruth, Ty Cobb, Christy Mathewson, Mickey Mantle, Denny McLain—as well as other luminaries who've come to town—Elvis, Sinatra, Liberace, Michael Jackson, the Beatles. Page eight is all Michael Jordan: a huge color caricature, a brief biography, a chart of his game-by-game fortunes so far, a sidebar about current prices on Jordan collectibles.

Michael would certainly appear to be the biggest thing to hit town since John, Paul, George, and Ringo.

One more thing on the sports page: the Bulls blew another fourth-quarter lead last night to go down 0–2 against the Knicks, and Horace Grant, back in "if territory," repeated, "If Michael was here, we'd be up 2–0." I wonder if the Barons' struggling .250 hitter secretly savors it, the guy who told *Chicago Tribune* writer and *Hang Time* author Bob Greene that he was always torn when he had to miss a Bulls game: "Part of me wants them to do well, part of me wants them to lose [to emphasize his importance]."

Wolfson Park sits beside the Gator Bowl, which is being renovated and expanded for the Jacksonville Jaguars' NFL debut in 1995. Two hours before the game, the place is abuzz, and not because it's Chamber of Commerce Night (free general admission for Chamber members and employees) and Elfin Evening (free general admission for fans presenting the package from any Keebler cookie, cracker, ice-cream cone or salty snack).

Program vendors bellow, "Michael Jordan's in the lineup! Get your prooo-gram here!" The merchandise-stands push T-shirts reading "Birmingham vs. Jacksonville, Wolfson Park, May 12, 13, 14, 1994" on the front, with Michael's number 45 on the back. A man named Jimmy Ballard from Coleman's Sporting Goods pumps out competing T-shirts at a temporary stand. The front reads, "Wolfson Park, Jacksonville vs. Birmingham, May 12–14, 1994," and pictures an anonymous black-jerseyed number 45 following through on a mighty swing (can't use Michael's likeness without paying!); the back says, "If you think he can't 'Just do it,' you've AIR'ed." Ballard says he cut a deal with Suns vice president Peter Bragan, Jr. to sell here in exchange for a percentage.

The sports directors from all the local TV stations are here doing on-the-scene spots for the evening news. ESPN's Steve Cyphers was around earlier, apparently. People from a couple of Japanese stations are here, only partly because the Jacksonville roster includes eighteen-year-old pitcher Makoto Suzuki.

In the press box, the *Times-Union* writers are saying they're sick of hearing about Michael Jordan, writing about Jordan, JordanJordanJordan. Normally one guy covers Suns games, but this evening they're all here: the beat writer, another sportswriter, the sports columnist, a news reporter, an editor, and two photographers.

———

Encountering Chris Pika in the press box, I smalltalk for a minute and then bring up the matter of some games I'd like to attend in Birmingham next week. I'm ignoring my conversation with Mister Falk, hoping Chris and I can pick up where we left off a week ago in Birmingham, when he was making nice.

No chance. Pika gives me the eye and says ominously, "We're still talking about your situation."

"But you said I could get in if I just let you know ahead of time."

"Yes, well . . ."

Believe It or Not

"Are you saying I'm going to have a hard time getting into home games?"

"Well, yes, I'd have to say you're not going to get credentials from us. Because you're not working for a legitimate news organization."

"I'm working for a reputable publisher."

"You're working for yourself. It's an unauthorized project. Look, it's my call, and I've talked to the White Sox PR people and they said they wouldn't give you access either."

"So it's your call or theirs? Or do you both get it from Mister Falk?"

"It's up to me," says Chris.

"How about Michael? He told me it's OK with him if I'm around and said he'd tell you. What did he tell you?"

The moment of truth. "Welll ... uhhh ... he said he'd rather not fool with it."

After Mister Falk told him not to fool with it, is my guess.

Or else he meant no all along and left it to the middlemen to break the news.

It hardly matters which. What's clear is that I'll have no access to Michael in Birmingham, where he plays half his games. I won't even be allowed into the press box to talk to people who do have access. I'm persona non grata with the Barons, entirely unwelcome, even if every other team in the Southern League (outside Huntsville) treats me like a king.

So I'll go over their heads, the simpletons. I'll go to the head of minor-league baseball, the head of major-league baseball, whatever it takes. Right will win out.

———

Wolfson Park keeps filling up through three innings, but the crowd reaches just 8,655—great for the Jacksonville Suns,

ROOKIE

averaging 3,100, but a thousand or two less than they expected for Michael.

"That's Jacksonville," one of the local writers remarks. "If this were a tractor pull or the World Wrestling Federation or Travis Tritt, this place would be packed."

It's another *slooow* minor-league game. The fans' attention drifts, zooms in when Michael comes to bat, then drifts again.

In the standing-room area down the right-field side, some sixth-graders spell out "Michael Jordan won't sign autographs" on the ground with peanut shells. But they say they understand. "We were going to say 'Michael stinks,' " one tells me, "but we didn't because we still like him."

Michael looks weak at the plate again. For what it's worth, he looks good in the field. He's made more errors than any Southern League outfielder, but chalk that up to inexperience; meanwhile, with those long, loping strides he covers a lot of territory. Naturally graceful, he makes the routine plays look good. He'll coast toward a lazy fly ball, camp under it and raise his glove as it descends (right hand dangling at his side), flex his knees slightly and then let the ball fall softly into the black mitt—no "Henderson snatch" at the end, nothing, just the most peaceful putting-away of a ball you can imagine.

At moments like this you can't help feeling, yet again, that the remarkable athleticism in those long limbs is sadly wasted here. You wish he'd go back to basketball while he's still got it.

He's got to think about it himself, after yet another whiff or feeble pop-up: *I could still be dominating the greatest players in the world in the greatest game of all!* He's got to have fleeting thoughts, at least, of going back next season. It would be natural for him to appreciate his game again, just as he understandably needed some time away from it. How sweet it would be for him (I would think) to come back next season and bring the Bulls back to the top. That's not a challenge?

———

With the score tied in the top of the ninth, Barons center fielder Kevin Coughlin reaches second base and Michael jolts a single to left center to knock in the go-ahead run. What's left of the crowd goes berserk, and when the Barons retire Jacksonville in the bottom of the ninth, Michael is the star of the game.

Just when you're thinking he should come to his senses and go home, he does something to make you wonder if he doesn't actually have the least little chance of making his baseball dream come true. You do know these moments will keep him coming back to the park a while longer.

———

Nearly an hour after the last out, several hundred people squeal from the railings when Michael, accompanied by Pika and five cops, returns to the field for his first-night-in-town press conference. The fans have gotten impatient in the last half hour, stomping their feet and chanting, "We want Michael! We want Michael!" even though they won't be able to get near him. They probably won't even be able to hear him talking to the press down near the third-base line, where there's a table set up as at Orlando.

The press is frustrated, too. Michael's a half hour late, deadlines have come and gone. Those without deadlines, well, we've got lives.

But Michael's been celebrating with his teammates, and who can blame him? Since we couldn't start without him, we who remain are simply glad when he does show up.

He's wearing baggy blue jeans with the cuffs rolled up, a

ROOKIE

sleeveless blue-denim shirt (long, powerful arms, a large gold watch), and light-brown suede shoes with no socks. The lights reflect off his pate. Sitting down in front of the microphone he gives us a glance and a little smile, the sign that someone may go ahead and start things off.

"How about your game-winning hit? Your first?"

"Naw, I had one before," Michael says casually, but he's not even trying to keep the smile off his face. It's sure not old stuff yet, like fifty-point playoff games.

When no one jumps in with another question, Michael expertly fills the lull by elaborating on his timely hit. "I think a pressure situation makes you concentrate even greater. I guessed curveball and stayed back and made good contact. From a mental standpoint, I've been in that situation many times before, but just not in this arena."

Was he surprised to get a curveball in that situation?

"Naw. I think everybody knows that's the weakest part of my game. I've adjusted to fastballs now, so pitchers are trying to get me out with curveballs and sliders."

When's he going to hit a homer?

"To be a long-ball hitter you've got to develop certain fundamentals and learn how to get bat speed—the hip turn, all that stuff. I've made gradual progress in terms of power, but I don't think I'm a long-ball hitter; I think I'm a base-hit hitter who utilizes my speed once I'm on the bases. I know the fans come out here wanting to see me knock it out of the park, but that's something that will come with time. You can't run before you walk."

Smooth, paint-by-numbers answers. Michael sits on the edge of the metal chair, too big for it, his muscled arms on the table, immense hands fingering the mike stand. He looks faintly bored, but he's fulfilling his obligation to his image, and thus to the companies he shills for. And knows how to do it:

Believe It or Not

keep it simple (let them read whatever they want into you), make eye contact with each questioner (add that personal touch), smile often (be a regular Joe).

He says that even as his average drops he's more comfortable all the time, moving away from the Hriniak method. Walt Hriniak, the White Sox batting coach, is a noted hitting guru whose method is taught throughout the organization. The method, which won Wade Boggs several batting titles when Hriniak was with the Boston Red Sox, is a repackaging of hitting fundamentals involving weight shift, a slight upper cut, and the early release of the top hand from the bat. Critics say it inhibits power and, like any style, is simply unnatural for some hitters.

"Walter gave me a great foundation in terms of getting myself in good hitting position," Michael says, "but Mike Barnett has helped me get more comfortable and let more of my natural ability come into my stance and my aggressiveness at the plate. I've always been the type of athlete who created my own style, and Mike Barnett has helped me find that style—feel comfortable at the plate, see the ball, react, move the ball all over the field. That's a major progression for me, and I think I can only get better."

Does he miss the adulation his basketball exploits brought? (Not that it's any less nowadays.)

"I don't miss it. The crowds have been very supportive of me here, and I've had my share of adulation over the years so that if I don't get any more, I know what it felt like. I'm not doing this for the adulation from the crowd."

Someone shouts, "How's the baseball life compared to the NBA?"

"A lot more fun, quite honestly. You have a lot more time to enjoy the camaraderieship that's in the game. In basketball you come in an hour and a half before the game, then you play and you're outta there in thirty, forty minutes. Here, I show up at two for a seven o'clock game, so you've got all that time to know your teammates. And that's fun. That's the kind of personality I've always had: I'm a people person; I like getting along with anybody.

"The bus rides have been great." He smiles, pauses, and we all laugh. "Long rides, but I can sleep anywhere. So I've enjoyed the whole experience. Naturally it's not your first-class flights in private jets, but this is how I started, you know, not with the luxuries of life. It fits me perfectly, although people don't think that."

And so on, and so on. When he's filled a fair amount of time, Pika steps in and wraps things up.

Some of the local guys are admittedly seduced. One remarks, "Did you notice how he looks right at you when he answers your question? You're thinking, 'Me and Michael, one-on-one. Yeah, I'm king of the world; I'm the man.' "

Another agrees, "It's a conscious thing, I know, probably something his agent tells him to do, but it works. And he's handsomer than I thought."

"I'd like to have his baby," the first one concludes—"if I could, that is."

———

Back at the motel I come upon an article about sports agents—focussing on Mister Falk, the Goliath—in the June *Playboy*. Jeff Coplon, whose basketball pieces have appeared in the *New Yorker* and the *New York Times Sunday Magazine*, hung out with Mister Falk before last year's NBA draft and describes him as "a power center unto himself, at the junction where gossip and commerce meet."

Coplon discovered that Mister Falk, a creature of the telephone, dislikes leaving phone messages. "If necessary, he will wait on hold for minutes at a time—not that he often has to.

Believe It or Not

He knows that few people in the rich, small world of the NBA will keep him waiting for long."

Mister Falk tells Coplon, "There are two worlds in the NBA—the media's world and the insider's world. It's good to feel you're on the inside."

Mister Falk, who humbly describes humbly named FAME as "a boutique for superstars," talks about the glut of "slimebuckets" in the agent business. In fact, he doesn't like being associated with agents—call him an attorney, please, like Michael does. (That's better?) Mister Falk has a clear conscience, considers himself a gentleman. (He did wish me luck on my book.) "Yet," Coplon writes, "for all of Falk's undisputed loyalty to his clients, for all of his carefully-sculpted self-promotion, he has an image problem. By reputation he is a man whose name is an expletive to NBA front offices, a hard case who would level his own grandmother if she blocked an accelerated payment schedule."

———

Poor Michael. His *life*. He chose it, of course—you don't become a conglomerate by accident—but what an existence: calling in to FAME a couple of times a day, countless calls *from* FAME, countless hours spent with Mister Falk over ten years and with countless others of his ilk, executives and deal-makers and schmoozers and money-men. Could he possibly *enjoy* that? Can it possibly be worth it to him, when he's long since earned enough money to support his family for any number of lifetimes? When, even with his life already out of control, the only point is to make him bigger?

Not out of control? A few years back he told an interviewer, "You do sacrifice a lot of your privacy. One of the things I miss is just being able to go out with my kids to an amusement park."

But he keeps making the sacrifice—sacrificing not only his

ROOKIE

trip to the amusement park, but his own kids' trip there with their dad. And whatall else?

In Thursday morning's *Times-Union*, columnist Tim McDonald allows as how he would gladly take Michael's bank account and fancy cars but wouldn't want any part of his life. "His fame has exploded into an abomination. It has surpassed the healthy stage. It's unnatural . . . A big percentage of the hordes who flock to see him are reacting to the fame, not to the man himself."

Not many of us, I suspect, actually *would* want Michael's life. He's rich and we're poor, but we're free. If we've got money to go the movies, we can go to the movies, no problem, no scene. We can go to our kids' Little League games and birthday parties.

We can read bedtime stories to our kids. We can be there watching them grow up, helping them grow up. Michael, all these years, has been on the road virtually all the time.

The "normal person" doesn't get the adulation from strangers that Michael gets, but a normal person doesn't need adulation.

If Michael doesn't need it, he apparently at least likes it. He's been called a prisoner of success, but becoming a prisoner of success is largely a matter of choice. Kareem Abdul-Jabbar, a phenomenon when he hit the pros in the 1970s, could have sculpted an image for the press and the advertisers, but decided he would rather be himself: scowl if he felt like scowling, take a political stand if so compelled. Larry Bird could have been huge in the mid-1980s but was happy being Bird.

Michael might be a prisoner of *celebrity*, a prisoner of his image, but he brought that on himself by abetting Mister Falk and Nike's Phil Knight and the rest of the money-men as they made him into a comic-book superhero.

Rights and
Responsibilities

"Better starve free than be a fat slave."
— Aesop, "The Dog and the Wolf," *Fables*

The past casts long shadows down here. Although I head west
out of Atlanta on the Ralph Abernathy Parkway and pass a
Martin Luther King Boulevard exit on the outskirts of town,
the drive to Birmingham takes me by Wedowee, Alabama,
where a high-school principal is in trouble for calling a biracial
student a "mistake" (the noted civil-rights lawyer Morris Dees
is representing her in a federal lawsuit) and for threatening to
cancel the prom rather than admit interracial couples.

In Birmingham the past is all around you. My motel is easy
walking distance from the classy Birmingham Civil Rights
Institute, which sits at Sixth Street and Sixteenth Avenue between beautiful Kelly Ingram Park, site of many demonstrations and confrontations, and the Sixteenth Avenue Baptist
Church, where three black children were killed in a notorious
1963 bombing. A plaque out in front of the Institute reads,
"Injustice anywhere is a threat to justice everywhere."

Inside, the tour begins with the stark, jolting reality of two
old water fountains sitting side by side—one marked "White,"
one "Colored."

ROOKIE

Next comes a whole wall of racist cartoons from old newspapers. Move on to revolting photographs of lynchings: young black men, hands bound, swinging from high limbs as giddy whites do everything but exchange highfives. The Klan. "Bull" Connor, Commissioner of Public Safety, with his firehoses and German shepherds.

As recently as 1963 (within weeks of Michael's birth in Brooklyn, New York), George Wallace was sworn in as governor of Alabama and called for "Segregation now, segregation tomorrow, segregation forever." Here in Birmingham a couple of kids named Dwight and Floyd Armstrong were denied entry to Graymont Elementary School by state troopers.

Yes, I know that Alabama and Mississippi have more black elected officials than any other states today, but I'm sick.

———

I wonder whether Michael has made the tour.

Ever so briefly, I wonder. His time is so tight—with ballgames and golf, with phone calls to and from FAME, with the dozen major companies he currently represents, with jewelers and financiers—I can't imagine when he'd fit it in. Besides, the mob scenes that await him in public must make it hardly worth going out except when one absolutely has to, say to play golf or shoot a commercial.

Most of all, Michael remains our preeminent pitchman by remaining politically and socially vanilla, so what's the sense in taking this tour and maybe getting riled up? An awakened social conscience can only confuse things.

In his excellent book *Days of Grace*, Arthur Ashe described his disappointment back in 1990 when Michael conspicuously avoided issuing public support for Harvey Gantt, a respected black politician who was challenging for Jesse Helms's Senate

Rights and Responsibilities

seat in Michael's home state of North Carolina. "For me, the main point is not that Gantt and Jordan are both black; rather, it is that Gantt's opponent, Jesse Helms, has a long history of supporting segregation, and the contest was close. For blacks across America, that Senate contest was the most important in decades . . . Jordan stuck to his apolitical position. 'I really don't know Gantt,' he said, in response to criticism of his silence. 'Well, Michael,' I would have told him, 'pick up the telephone and call him!' A few appearances with Gantt might well have made the difference. Instead, Helms returned to the Senate."

After the Los Angeles riots in 1992, even Michael's teammate Craig Hodges noted Michael's reticence. "When they came to Michael after the L.A. deal went down and asked him what he thought, his reply was that he really wasn't up on what was going on. I can understand that, but at the same time, that's a bailout situation, because you are bailing out when some heat is coming on you. We can't bail anymore.

"Leadership in America is the athletes and entertainers," Hodges went on, stretching a point to make a point. "On the one hand, being in this league, you have a right to make as much as you can. But you have a responsibility. A lot of us don't look at the responsibility end of it as much as we do our right to ask for as much as we can get."

Black activists question Michael's empathy, to say the least. Robert Lucas, president of Chicago's Kenwood-Oakland Community Organization, was quoted in Jim Naughton's *Taking to the Air* as saying Michael had turned his back on the legacy of past black sports heroes in exchange for "crossover" status, the ability to pitch products as effectively to whites as to blacks. "People didn't idolize Joe Louis because he had a sharp jab and a hell of a right hand. We idolized Joe Louis because at least we saw him beating up white folk who were our oppressors. Jackie Robinson, he dared to do what white folks didn't want him to. He could have been a .250 hitter and we would have idolized him. Muhammad Ali, we saw him as much as a fighter for blacks as he was in the ring. You can't put Jordan in with those people. Jordan is symbolic at best."

Chicago actor and political satirist Aaron Freeman told Naughton, "[Jordan] and the other 'model Negroes' achieve this *transcendental irrelevance*. When people are trying to get the mayor to do something, maybe on affordable housing, no one calls Michael Jordan to be part of the movement. There are no illusions about him. He's not going to fight for your rights or your job or anything.

"He's not a hero, but he plays one on TV."

Michael's lifelong friend Fred Whitfield said, "Most of these major corporations can't afford to have [Michael] be too controversial."

Barbara Allen said, "He's made it clear to me he is going to stay away from any and all political events."

I'm still disappointed that Michael didn't come out for gun control after his father's murder last summer. I sent him a letter in care of the Bulls last fall: *Your critics say you're nothing more than a jock when you could be much more. This is a perfect opportunity to be more. People can relate to this tragedy. Hook up with a senator, make some gun-control ads, make a speech, whatever.*

I didn't expect anything. Lots of good consumers pack rods, and you don't offend good consumers.

Now I read that Michael's response to his dad's murder was to purchase a couple of handguns.

———

Reading Bob Greene's informative but idolatrous 1992 bestseller *Hang Time* ("Diabetics beware," one critic cautioned),

Rights and Responsibilities

I'm struck by the casual way Greene and Michael himself talk about what many would call selling out. Greene writes that due to Michael's "acceptance that his commercial endorsements were based upon his image of being amiable and accessible, he was careful any time he was in public not to appear curt, or short-tempered, or discourteous to strangers . . . He seemed to understand that part of the bargain he had made with life was that he would be held to a higher standard of comportment than the rest of the world."

I wonder if Michael, by now, has any idea who he is and how he really feels about things. Back around 1991 he was telling Greene, "I like to be considered a good person. I hope that I am. But I also realize that from the marketability standpoint, I really don't have any choice anymore. That's all gone, having that choice. I can't do things or say things that maybe other people can. I accept that—it's a choice I made, and the rewards are great, and I live with that choice."

Others do, too. Michael felt compelled to make a public apology after testifying in federal court in 1992 that he had indeed written a check for $57,000 to one "Slim" Bouler, who was being tried on drug-related charges. Michael said the check was to pay off golf bets, and knowing what we know of Michael's golf, it probably was. But the association with Bouler didn't look great, and Michael issued an apology assuring his public that one thing he'd learned was, "I shouldn't gamble with goons."

Of course, he didn't seem to mind hanging out and gambling with "goons" so much as getting caught at it and possibly sullying his goldmine of an image. At that point, he was ready to defame a crony.

Since Michael presumably has enough dough to last forever, several million times over, one wonders when it became a

ROOKIE

matter of piling up absolutely as much as he could, whatever the sacrifice. Friends? "Goons," if they made him look bad. Family life? In Naughton's *Taking to the Air*, Michael's "scheduler"—Barbara Allen!—said, "He is fully booked from the end of the [NBA] playoffs through October 1 [shortly before fall camp]."

But Michael keeps at it, and because he's only in the first part of most of his long-term, big-bucks advertising contracts, we'll be seeing him well into the next century as the down-home superstar, redolent of innocence and virtue, playing professional baseball or basketball or Ping-Pong or golf and playing with kids on playgrounds in his free time—even as, in real life, he retreats behind bodyguards and twelve-foot walls and pistols, and signs ever fewer autographs when he's out in public.

I don't get it. I'm reminded of the scene in *Key Largo* when the old coot asks Edward G. Robinson's classic gangster, Johnny Rocco, why he's doing these bad things, what's he after? Rocco is stumped—until Bogart steps in and tells the roomful, "I'll tell you what he wants. He wants *more*—isn't that right, Rocco?" Rocco brightens, as if it's a great concept: "Yeahhh, that's it—*more*. That's right, I want *more*."

Bogart asks, "Will you ever get enough?" and Edward G. replies, "Well, I never have. No, I guess I won't."

Country Roads

"Take all away from me, but leave me Ecstasy
And I am richer than all my fellow men."

— Emily Dickinson

On Tuesday night, May 17, I pay my way into Hoover Stadium and watch Michael go 1-for-8 and get caught stealing as the Barons split a doubleheader with the Greenville Braves.

Not surprisingly, Michaelmania seems to be ebbing, at least in Birmingham. After all, once you've laid eyes on him, then what? Fans can't get close to him, and from a distance he's just a struggling minor-league ballplayer.

He's not even mentioned in the *News'* game story on Wednesday. Two weeks ago, every account was worked around him. On the day after a kid named Mike Robertson was the hitting star and Michael impotent, the first two-thirds of the game story was another description of M.J.'s phenomenal (basketball) feats and money and fame, leading to the conclusion that everyone wants to "be like Mike." Followed by the punch line, "Mike Robertson, that is," and a few words about Robertson's lusty performance.

But it's changing. The beat writers have gotten used to having Michael around. He's there, that's all, and they've gotten comfortable with the idea that even though he's Michael

ROOKIE

Jordan, he's also just a guy, much like themselves … who happened to play astonishing basketball.

———

The Bulls have fought back to tie their series with the bullyboy Knicks at two games each, and you can't help thinking how nice it would be if the peerless one were there, thrilling us as he put the loathesome New Yorkers in their place. During the fourth game, NBC showed some highlights of Chicago's clincher over Ewing & Co. last spring—Michael sinking incredible stop-on-a-dime jumpers and slithering to the hole for tomahawks—and I wished I could ask him if he misses it. (Under truth serum.)

———

On a beautiful Wednesday evening, May 18, Michael goes 0-for-4 to drop to .231, down from .333 three weeks ago. Attendance is 4,724—not bad for a weeknight, not bad for any minor-league game, but smaller than before.

———

On Thursday, May 19, author Michael Jordan's picture appears alongside *USA Today*'s best-seller list. *I Can't Accept Not Trying*, "a little book with inspiring words," is at number 66.

Little, it is: for twelve bucks, it's a three-minute read, not counting the time you'll sit pondering such highlighted wisdom as "Fear is an illusion"; "There are no shortcuts"; and "The minute you get away from fundamentals, the bottom can fall out."

———

Country Roads

Still struggling in his relationship with the pitched ball, Michael is down to .221 when the Nashville Xpress come to town on May 24.

Michaelmania isn't manic anymore, but people still line the right-field railing when the Barons come out to warm up: tonight's "Field Of Dreams" Little Leaguers, some teenagers, a few adults. The kids are holding the usual balls, gloves, programs, cards, and posters in hand, though they know by now that Michael rarely signs. Mostly they're down there for a closer look; the grown-ups tag along to take their (and Michael's) picture.

Chris Pika scurries around in his Barons shirt and baggy khakis and brand-new Nikes (naturally). He's got his walkie-talkie, but he can't find anything more vital to do than show a local TV cameraman where to set up.

A hefty bearded fellow and a hefty bleached blonde, the "morning team" from WZZK, throw out the ceremonial first balls. The PA man announces that proceeds from tonight's game will be split between Michael Jordan charities and a couple of local ones.

I watch from the first row behind the Barons' first-base dugout. Three thirtyish guys nearby who've had a few beers are having fun with Nashville's huge and jovial hitting instructor, Frank Funderburk, who coaches down at first when the Xpress are at bat. "Stay in the box!" they keep yelling at him, and to the base umpire, "Watch him, blue!" Funderburk laughs; I laugh. "Hey! He's out of the box again, blue! Watch him!" The next inning, one guy calls him "Puckett." (The Xpress is a Minnesota Twins farm team, and Kirby Puckett of the Twins, though shorter than Funderburk, has a similarly sizable rump.) His buddy calls, "You know Kirby?" Funderburk turns and says, "I wish I had his money."

ROOKIE

Everyone has his own style. The moment the Xpress are retired each inning, Barons batting coach Mike Barnett, who like Funderburk doubles as first-base coach, pops out of the dugout and heads for the coaching box in his pigeon-toed, tippytoe gait. From there, in good baseball tradition, he chats up the Nashville first baseman, who's flipping grounders to the infielders while the pitcher warms up. But "Barney," as he's familiarly known, is all business as soon as a batter steps in. "C'mon, Dougie!" he calls to second baseman Doug Brady. (Baseball men add "ie" to players' names whenever possible, as in Jimmie, Timmie, Tommie.) He hunches forward for each pitch, hands on knees, intently studying pitcher and hitter. As soon as the ball hits the catcher's mitt he releases from his stance and straightens up, daintily expelling a spray of spittle. Then, like everyone else in the park, he kills time until the pitcher toes the rubber again—at which point Barnett faces the plate and drops into hands-on-knees position, peering in so intently you'd think the meaning of life was to be revealed in this next pitch.

Michael, at bat, is still "making adjustments." He's got his bat up off his shoulder again, in a position more like most hitters. Makes sense. Down in Florida, Barnett told me that laying the bat on your shoulder eliminates a step because you don't start your actual swing from up high—you drop your hands, *then* come through—but you don't start from on your shoulder, either.

Maybe it's desperation. It looks as if Michael is thinking, *Screw it, I'm not hitting anything with these esoteric mechanics, I'm just gonna go after the ball.*

But he looks a mess. His anxiety about striking out is at odds with the need to be patient and wait for a pitch he can handle. On almost any pitch that looks like a strike coming out of the pitcher's hand, Michael starts—too early—and if it's a curveball, he's finished; his swing is committed to a certain spot well before the ball hooks.

He's frustrated to the point of beefing over a called strike *two* in the sixth inning. He can't afford to give up a strike, any strike.

He does manage an infield single on the next pitch and promptly steals second. Something to keep him coming back.

———

Skimming *Baseball Weekly*, I come across a little item about a new Michael Jordan baseball card coming out soon, an artist's conception of Michael for some kind of special set. "Jordan—through agreements with Upper Deck, Major League Baseball Properties and his agent David Falk—was not allowed to appear in any other company's set, other than Upper Deck, before May 1."

———

I savor the long drives on the backroads on these long summer days, one Southern League town to the next: the tang of roadside honeysuckle and magnolia in the long stretches of country, the fillin' stations where the screen door creaks when you open it and bangs shut behind you, the Mayberryish communities where languid locals in pickups say howdy by lifting an index finger off the steering wheel—as slow, as mellow, as hospitable as can be . . .

But the sunny, happy, honeysuckle-scented roads that seem so friendly by day feel pregnant with peril when you come through at 2 A.M. You think back on the smiling faces you saw all day, recall the friendly accents ("Y'all raht?"), but out here in the black middle of the night you're checking your gas gauge, wondering if you've got a spare tire, praying you don't have a breakdown, because anyone you encounter out here at this hour is more likely to resemble the redneck hicks in *Easy Rider* or *Cool Hand Luke*, with nasty accents and nastier intentions, than any beatific Mayberry type.

But that tinge of dread is part of the experience, and you cruise, alone with your thoughts and your life, savoring the freedom. You pull into a truck stop or a Waffle House out in the middle of nowhere and order something good and greasy and eavesdrop on the waitresses and truckers and real-life Americans you find in a Waffle House in the middle of nowhere in the middle of a summer night down South. You think, *Michael can't do this—can't be free and can't be anonymous.* Back on the road again, the tunes blaring, a never-before-noticed riff by Al Green or Marvin Gaye suddenly brings you to tears . . .

———

I don't expect a huge crush for Michael's second swing through Nashville, "Tune Town," where billboards promote Loretta Lynn's Country Stores and Twitty City and the Grand Old Opry. Stars aren't as scarce here as in other Southern League venues, and Michael, down to .214 and striking out nearly a third of the time, might not be a big draw. In today's *Nashville Banner*, the only mention of him is on page five in the sports section.

The story rehashes the Barons' first visit, a month ago, when Michael was hitting .330 and the Nashville Xpress, playing in the Southern League's largest park, totaled 33,694 customers for two games. Some 3,000 fans remained for forty-five minutes after the first game, hoping for an autograph or at least a glimpse. In fifteen other home dates so far, the Xpress have

Country Roads

averaged less than 1,000 per game; Michael's two appearances bump the season average to 2,716.

Out at Greer Stadium, long before game time, the PR man lets me in through a gate not far from where Michael and a couple of teammates are taking turns in a batting cage behind the stands. The PR man quickly lets me know that Michael, who's swinging a weighted bat outside the cage a few feet away, is off-limits right now, and all night.

But whether it's because Michael is a .214 hitter or because the citizens of Nashville thought it would be impossible to get a ticket, nearly everyone stays home tonight. The announced attendance is 5,083, but attendance figures always include season tickets, whether or not their holders attend. This alleged 5,083 looks especially measly in spacious Greer Stadium.

The game is uneventful, at least Michaelwise: 0-for-4, one strikeout. He's at .209. I won't look for a big crowd tomorrow.

But on Friday night, more than 10,000 turn out and see Michael produce a single in three tries.

Saturday night, more than 11,000 watch as an 0-for-3 drops him to .207—ever closer to the dread "Mendoza Line," a .200 batting average.

Michael's skid has meant a rebirth of sorts for a former shortstop named Mario Mendoza—although reporters find Mendoza, retired since 1982, unhappy to be linked with Michael. After all, Mendoza acquired his dubious fame in the major leagues, not Double A, and though he finished below .200 four times in nine seasons, he had a .215 lifetime average. One wag, in Mendoza's defense, points out that it should properly be called the Uecker Line: Bob Uecker, the former catcher and beer pitchman and occasional sitcom star, batted exactly .200 over his six-year major-league career.

———

ROOKIE

I zap off a fax to the Baseball Writers Association of America, describing my tribulations in Birmingham.

They zap one right back saying they have no control over accreditation in minor-league parks and giving me the name of someone at minor-league headquarters in St. Petersburg.

Travis Tritt twangs "Here's a Quarter (Call Someone who Cares)" as I head out of Nashville . . .

You Gotta Dream

*"Ah, but a man's reach should exceed his grasp,
Or what's a heaven for?"*

— Robert Browning, "Andrea Del Sarto,"
Men and Women

The radio issues more gospel and blues and less truck-stop country with every passing burg on the backroads from Chattanooga west to Memphis. A billboard at a turnoff—a huge Jack Daniel's label—lets me know the famous distillery is a few miles up the road, but I stay on course ... past long, long cornfields, and long country yards where an old man in a straw hat or a young wife in a sundress picks vegetables in a dense garden; through country stretches where stately old trees hang over the road and sunlight splinters down through the leaves; through the next faceless speck on the map, shaking my head and thinking, *Yeah, people actually live out here*, even though there's scarcely a living soul in sight, except for a few hound dogs, on Sunday afternoon. Until you get to the Wal-Mart plaza—where, in burg after burg, the parking lot is packed.

I'm thinking about Michael. I see him going back to the NBA. I picture him heading back to the Barons' dugout after yet another weak groundout, the crowd cheering nonetheless—it's got to feel a little odd. A guy who's used to being the one and only has got to be frustrated, struggling in

ROOKIE

Double-A ball while youngsters like Frank Thomas and Ken Griffey Jr. toy with big-league pitching much as Michael toyed with the NBA. People play games to have fun, and being Michael on the basketball court would seem to be more amusing than struggling, at age thirty-one, to keep your minor-league batting average above .200.

And he needs to stay in the public eye—for all those lucrative long-term endorsements, if not for his ego. I don't see his baseball career lasting much beyond this season, but if Michael is contracted to shill well into the twenty-first century he can't just drop out of sight. What else is there but hoops? Mister Falk always said Michael could go into politics or something, like they all say, but let's be serious.

———

Like every Southern League town the first time Michael comes through, Memphis is jazzed. The Chicks, whose numerous investors include Ron Howard and Bob Costas, anticipate three sellouts and have tripled security personnel. They'll be operating twenty-two concession stands instead of the usual eight. Gates will open early so the fans can see Michael's batting-practice swings. The game will start an hour early so that reporters with 10 P.M. deadlines can get Michael's press conference into their accounts.

Tim McCarver Stadium was renamed a few years ago for the local boy who made good as a big-league catcher, then as an announcer, and who also owns a piece of the Chicks these days. Whether it's the intermittent rain or Michael's .207 average, there's not much activity outside when I arrive two hours before gametime. As at every stop, a few people are gaping at the Barons' famous bus as if it might turn a cartwheel or take flight, but there aren't many cars in the lot, no lines at the ticket windows. I pick up my press pass and breeze in.

You Gotta Dream

As always, most of the early arrivals are bunched in the first few rows of the right-field bleachers. In front of them, on the grass in foul territory, a half-dozen photographers focus on Michael, who's out in right field awaiting his turn in batting practice.

When he starts jogging in, the photographers move en masse, cameras raised, snapping pictures as they backpedal. Michael, encountering a lonely baseball lying on the grass near the foul line, picks it up without breaking stride and flips it behind his back, into the clot of kids at the railing—drawing an ovation, naturally. Like that beautiful woman who needs only say hello to make you swoon.

As he loosens up behind the cage, the photographers cluster a few feet away, frantically clicking close-ups while the opportunity exists. Pika hovers nearby and eagerly scolds anyone who strays over his imaginary line. Michael, lazily swinging his black bat with a weight on the end, pretends none of them exist.

There's a big ovation and the familiar focus of attention when he steps in to whack at Terry Francona's lollipops. It's as if the game just started.

When he completes his first half-dozen swings and jogs to first, the fans on that side cheer as if he'd just smacked a bases-loaded triple. He idles on to second, eventually passes it, and idles on toward third—where, as he approaches, the people behind that dugout carry on as if he were sliding in with that three-bagger.

When he puts one (barely) over the left-field fence the second time around, you'd think the blast had won the World Series.

———

I chat with Chicks president Dave Hersh, whom I remember as the twentysomething owner of the Portland Beavers back in

ROOKIE

the early 1980s, with a slick line of patter and a big cigar in hand. He's flattered that I remember and likes being joshed that he's still a legend in Portland. Hersh later put in some time with the New York Yankees under George Steinbrenner, an unhappy interlude, and wound up in Memphis. He's still glib and smooth, still got a stogie in his hand. Loves the Memphis job, but sure, he'd like to be back in the big leagues someday.

Ron Johnson, the Chicks' thirty-eight-year-old manager, is among the curious watching Michael take BP, but like everyone else he's preoccupied with his own life and prospects. Briefly a Kansas City Royal in the early 1980s, Johnson managed Royals Single-A teams the last two years (Wilmington, North Carolina and Baseball City, Florida). He's not satisfied with reaching Double A.

"When I got a chance in managing and coaching, I made it very clear that I wanted to go to the big leagues. That's my goal, whether as a coach or a manager. I'm not a guy who'll be content being a career minor-league guy.

"I think maybe for some guys, say a guy who's had a long career in the big leagues, it's not the same thing. Take U. L. Washington [the fit-looking Chicks' coach who's a few feet away slapping grounders to the infielders]. Wash played eleven years in the big leagues. He enjoys working with young players; he's an outstanding teacher—I don't think his aspirations to go back to the big leagues are as great as mine. I had a hundred days up there."

For now, all Johnson knows for sure is that, with a two-year contract, he'll be managing somewhere in the Royals' organization next season. Johnson married a secretary from Orlando two days before spring training this year ("twenty-eight years old, five-foot-nine, blonde—*wooooooooo!*"), having warned her that baseball is an unstable life. This summer she's keeping her

You Gotta Dream

job in Orlando and visiting him occasionally at his apartment in Memphis. They'll winter in Orlando: she'll keep her job and Johnson, who likes to pump iron, will look for a job in a gym. Next season, wherever he goes, she's going with him. Beyond, who knows?

The baseball life, minor-league version.

How about tonight's main attraction? Johnson, who set a Southern League record with forty doubles for the Chicks in 1980 but managed only 12-for-46 in twenty-two big-league games, with no homers and no RBI, is doubtful about Michael's chances.

"As far as whether he can develop into a major-league star, in my opinion that's very hard to do. Especially for a guy who's already thirty-one years old. I'm grooming guys who are twenty-one and twenty-two to play another two or three years to get to their primes, to get to the big leagues. A gentleman who's already thirty-one . . . what he's gonna do, play two or three years in the minors and then go to the big leagues?

"He's got a long way to go offensively. It's a long shot. But who knows?" Johnson laughs. "I wouldn't bet against the guy. I was a Chicago Bulls fan."

Behind the batting cage I meet the Barons' pleasant, diminutive pitching coach, Kirk Champion. On one level, Champion is simply happy to be making a living in professional baseball. After playing college ball at Southwest Missouri State University, he managed to avoid the real world by staying on as an assistant coach at SMSU, then head-coaching at Rend Lake (Illinois) Community College, then moving to Southern Illinois University as an assistant before being invited, at age thirty, to join the White Sox organization. He's thirty-six now, and though he may or may not ever reach the majors, he may never have to look for a real job, either.

ROOKIE

Then again, minor-league life is hardly the end-all, with the low pay and the seasonal rentals and the time away from your family. Yes, Kirk Champion wants to move up. "That's why we're all out here, right?"

———

After BP and infield practice, the Barons retire to their clubhouse, vanishing through a gate down in the right-field corner. A few minutes before game time, in twos and threes, they make the long walk back. Michael comes last, accompanied by a teammate and two security cops. The hordes hanging over the railing, who've ignored the rest of the passing Barons, go nuts. Michael, near enough to feel the vibrations from their screaming in his eardrums, pretends not to notice.

Near the first-base dugout, one teenage girl in a group of three studies the approaching idol through a pair of binoculars. "He doesn't look as happy as he does in his commercials," she reports to her friends.

Showers or no, 10,000-seat McCarver Stadium has nearly filled up by the time the Chicks hit the field and we rise for the national anthem. The eventual crowd of 9,842 is the biggest of the season here and the fourteenth-biggest ever (after such extravaganzas as a Royals' exhibition game a few years back, an appearance by the "Famous Chicken," and various Hat Nights and other promotions). Michael continues to fill Southern League coffers: the average attendance of 8,072 at Barons games, home and road, is more than double the league average and one of the all-time minor-league highs.

We're joined in the press box this evening by Michael's pal Bob Greene from the *Chicago Tribune*. Any pal of Michael's, of course, takes on a certain stature by association, and Chris Pika can't do enough for Greene even though, as visiting flack, he's not really on duty to the press.

You Gotta Dream

Michael, batting in the first inning with the bases loaded and two outs, looks especially bad in the course of striking out. The rains come soon afterward, forcing a lengthy delay. When the skies clear, leaving us a beautiful, breezy evening, and the huge tarp has been rolled up and bags of sand raked into the muck around the bases, Michael comes up in the third inning and whiffs again. Third time up, he looks futile on a couple of swings before managing a groundout to the shortstop. He looks as if he's losing his spirit a little.

Greene and I chat. He's interested in hearing about any book about his friend. "Hard or soft?" he asks of mine, and then some questions about my publisher, deadline, publication date, and so forth.

When I describe my difficulty getting near Michael—that is, Mister Falk's attempt to bleed me—Greene says, "What do you expect? Falk's an agent. If Michael doesn't get anything, Falk doesn't get anything."

He pays closer attention to the game when I suggest that Michael is accountable for his representatives.

It's a tight, well-played game, the Barons trailing 2–1 going into the ninth inning. It comes down to runners on first and third with two outs, Michael coming to the plate. Ron Johnson pops out of the Chicks' dugout and walks to the mound, takes the ball from his pitcher, and signals to the bullpen for the right-hander Jimmy Myers. The organist plays a jaunty tune as Michael stands a few feet from the plate studying the reliever's warm-up pitches.

Myers throws four fastballs. Strike. Ball. Lame swing for strike two, Michael seemingly looking for the curveball. And a lame swing for the whiff, fooled again. Barons lose.

Worse, Michael is perilously close to the Mendoza Line at .202.

ROOKIE

Thirty minutes later, two dozen reporters and cameramen fill a conference room in the Chicks' offices behind the left-field fence, waiting for Michael to show up for his one-time-only press conference.

Outside, cops keep a throng of kids back. Over in the right-field corner, where Michael should be emerging any minute (he's already late), dozens of kids hang over the railings, each hoping to be the first to spot him.

Time passes. Chicks president Dave Hersh puffs on his ubiquitous cigar and, though he himself keeps glancing out the window toward that gate in right field, tries to distract the impatient press with jokes and anecdotes. Hersh wants things to go smoothly; tonight's a big night. As one wag cracks, pointing to the table at the front where the guest of honor will sit, "I'll bet that's a picture you never thought you'd see: an ESPN microphone and a Memphis Chicks cap in the same frame."

For all his worldliness, Hersh is one more human who, from afar, sees nearly superhuman virtues in Michael. He winds up a glowing description of Michael's "work ethic" and "character" by saying what a "class guy" he is. I can't resist asking Dave how much time he's spent around Michael. Very little, he admits.

While the restless reporters propose an award for whoever asks the most asinine question tonight, the increasingly edgy Hersh makes the long walk across the outfield to find out what's going on. A few minutes later we see his lonely figure making the long walk back. The word: "I've been assured he's coming. Hopefully soon."

But the people with 10 P.M. deadlines have already left, out of luck.

Finally, an hour and twenty minutes after Michael's whiff

ended the game, someone says, "Here he comes," and a bull-pen cart with three figures in it moves out of the shadows in the right-field corner and comes around the warning track toward us.

But as the cart approaches, with no famous pate shining under the lights, dismayed voices start murmuring, "That's not Michael Jordan." When the cart stops, a dumpy figure in baggy khakis and new Nikes steps out and there's only the sad fact, "That's Chris Pika!" Coming, obviously, to extend Michael's regrets.

Sure enough, a grim Pika comes in and addresses us like a White House flack announcing a matter most grave. "Ladies and gentlemen, I've just talked to Michael Jordan, and Mr. Jordan would like me to say that, being a team player, he's very disappointed in his performance tonight, and he hopes that you ladies and gentlemen of the media will understand that he doesn't feel like coming over here tonight. Thank you."

Someone shouts, "Does that mean he'll do it tomorrow night?"

"I can't say. I don't know." Poor Chris is already backing out the door, sensing the possibility of a stoning.

When he's gone, a local wit remarks, "Michael's going to let his bat do his talking. Unfortunately, he's the Helen Keller of the Southern League."

———

Back at McCarver Stadium on Tuesday, ponytailed pop star Michael Bolton and his "Bolton Bombers" destroy a squad of local deejays in a two-inning softball game following the Chicks' and Barons' warm-ups. When the pros return, I catch Barons batting coach Mike Barnett down on the field.

"Everybody is caught up in Michael's average right now,"

the amiable Barnett says, "but for someone who hasn't played baseball in fourteen years, he has held his own at the plate. And he's starting to drive the ball better. We're not concerned about batting average. Sure he'd like to be hitting .330, but the big thing is where he is a month from now, two months, three months. We want him to be swinging the bat good at the end of the year so we can make a good evaluation of where he's at."

Memphis first baseman Dan Rohrmeier, the Southern League's latest Player of the Week, sympathizes with Michael's struggles. Says Rohrmeier, originally drafted by the White Sox in 1987, "I never embraced the Walt Hriniak theories of hitting, which is what the organization teaches you. I had to hit that way for a couple of years and I hated it. I think Michael Jordan should swing like Michael Jordan. I'd love to talk to him, because I know what he's going through."

In the press box, the locals dog Pika about whether Michael's going to do a press conference after tonight's game.

Pika doesn't know. "He only promises one the first night in every city."

"But he blew us off last night."

"I don't know."

The Chicks, incidentally, win their eleventh in a row at home as a crowd of 9,762 sees Michael put up an uneventful 1-for-4. Michael isn't sufficiently pleased to meet the press afterward.

We can only pray he'll speak tomorrow.

———

Wednesday evening, Michael, apparently hoping to change his luck, has changed his look. Usually he's got his pants pulled all the way down his spindly shins, disappearing into his hightop shoes, but tonight he turns them under just below the knee to reveal the black stirrup socks and the white sanitary hose underneath—like players wore them until recent years, but exaggeratedly so. Maybe someone told him his strike zone will look smaller to the umpire.

Six people wearing Event Staff T-shirts hang around the Barons' dugout while Michael relaxes after his batting-practice cuts. When he finally moves back out to right field, they drift along behind him as if they're expecting the first-graders along the railing to hop over, sprint out and attack him.

I approach Terry Francona. Down in Florida, a few days after meeting his wife at Hoover Stadium, I had asked him about getting together for an interview. I wanted to hear about Michael, yes, but I figured Francona's story itself would be illuminating: son of a major leaguer, a major leaguer himself, minor-league manager, minor-league Manager of the Year, aspiring major-league manager. Francona was friendly and told me to get back to him.

Alas, Terry must have seen me on a wanted poster in the meantime. He's chilly saying hello and grimaces when I ask about getting together to talk. He says, "Your book is un-authorized, right?"

That word! (Mister Falk!)

"Michael told me it was OK with him," I say, exasperated. "I think maybe his *agent* doesn't like the idea."

Terry's eyes dart around as if he's afraid someone will see him talking to me. "I don't know if I should talk to you. I don't think Michael is too hepped-up about the idea. Tell you what—let me talk to Michael. If it's OK with him, I'll give you all the time you want."

"Look, I'm not only interested in Michael. I'd like to find out about growing up with a big-league father, your playing career, managing, minor-league life."

ROOKIE

Terry's nodding. "Let me talk to Michael. If it's OK with him, I'll give you all the time you want. I'm not trying to be a hardass."

Crazy. A nice guy, Francona, but come on.

Unauthorized. Someone tells them that, pronouncing the word with a certain attitude, and they start looking at you like you smell bad—like you reek figuratively, at least, with the moral stench of your sleazy endeavor.

———

With the press box packed, I watch the first few innings in the radio booth with Tom Stocker, "voice of the Chicks" for eight years and the 1988 Southern League Announcer of the Year.

Jordan? "Not a baseball player," Stocker asserts. "He has to think about things these other guys do instinctively. He looks as out of place here as the other guys would look in Madison Square Garden."

"But he's down here to learn, right?"

"That's right. He'll be here as long as the White Sox think he might do something someday. Until they decide it's a joke."

As the Barons take the field after being retired in the top of the first, their voice and triviameister Curt Bloom passes through our booth on his way to pick up a soda and tells his counterpart Stocker, "We [the Barons] haven't had a one-two-three first inning by a starting pitcher since May 17—fourteen games. Since *May 17.*"

Two minutes later, with the second Chicks' hitter at the plate, Tom Stocker regurgitates C.B.'s factoid into the airwaves: "The last time a Birmingham starting pitcher had a one-two-three first inning was May 17. The Barons have gone *almost half a month* without retiring the side in order in the first."

———

You Gotta Dream

Michael, 0-for-4 with three groundouts and a whiff, drops below .200 for the first time and again refuses to do a press conference. So much for Memphis.

The rest of the Barons leave on the famous bus after the game and roll into Birmingham at four in the morning. Michael takes a midnight flight so he gets a good night's sleep before his 8 A.M. tee-off in a charity golf tournament with Charles Barkley, Lee Trevino, and Arnold Palmer, among others. Five armed police officers trot alongside the cart that carries Michael and Barkley around the course.

After playing golf most of the day, Michael manages a single in four tries against the Carolina Mudcats. After the game, Barkley and football star Cornelius Bennett and "about ten of their closest, most raucous friends," according to the next morning's paper, carry on in the Barons' clubhouse.

Diamond Dig

"We must believe in the gods no longer if injustice is to prevail over justice."

— Euripides, *Electra*

On June 6 I send a fax to Mike Moore, president of minor-league baseball, explaining my problems with the Barons. They can't get away with it . . . can they?

By now, I'm not so sure.

———

Michael, discussing his struggles with a reporter, says, "I've learned this game comes in stages. First it was fastballs; nobody thought I could hit fastballs. When I got to the fastballs they started throwing me off-speed stuff. It's just a matter of me seeing enough of those pitches, getting used to them, and being able to excel in hitting them."

He admits his confidence has been shaken. "Yeah, it suffered a little bit. I've never been through anything like this before. It's frustrating. You know what you want to do but you can't do it."

As for the pants, worn of late in the old-fashioned style, "It's the Negro League look, a change of attitude. I saw some other guys doing it. It's a new month, so a new look. It's been good to me," he adds, claiming he's made better contact lately—for instance, the ringing double to the left–center-field gap on

Diamond Dig

Saturday night. "I'm on the way back up. I'm making contact and I'm not striking out as much. They're all good signs for me."

Batting-coach Mike Barnett says, "His average has gone down, but he's actually a better hitter now than he was during his thirteen-game hitting streak."

———

But his progress is slow to the point of imperceptible. Against the Huntsville Stars on June 6 he looks overmatched again, but a sympathetic official scorer bumps him up to .200 by giving him a base hit when the shortstop fields his grounder and throws wide of first.

Michael, who's among the league leaders in steals only because he tries so often, promptly gets thrown out going for second.

He's also made more errors than any Southern League out-fielder. Tonight, with a Star on first base, he cruises in to pick up a ground-ball single, plays it casual, and muffs it, allowing the runner to blow around second base and on to third.

Late-night *SportsCenter* goes to a commercial promising to update Michael's fortunes: "Highlights, if you will, when we return."

———

But the kids still worship him. Headline over a *USA Today* story, June 7: "Jordan packs 'em in; fans flock to see a sub-.200 hitter." The piece quotes Jake Rimington of Birmingham, five-year-old right fielder for the Dave's Discount Drugs Blue Jays, who got to take the field with Michael recently in the pregame "Field of Dreams" promotion: "Very awesome. His hand is pretty strong."

ROOKIE

Spence Tribble, thirteen, got Michael's autograph on his copy of *I Can't Accept Not Trying* and then sealed the volume in a plastic freezer-bag. He says, "I'm going to frame it, the whole book. I feel excited—and relieved. I've been trying for so long."

Even some adults are still rendered breathless. Chris Pika, quoted for the umpteenth time during his fifteen minutes of fame, says he won't ask Michael for an autograph. "He's already autographed my career. No matter where I go for the rest of my life, that will always be part of it—I worked with Michael Jordan."

And team president Bill Hardekopf tells the *Birmingham News*, "He's a fun-loving, gregarious guy. Here's the world's greatest athlete, playing with guys eight or nine years younger than him who aren't on his financial level. He participates in Kangaroo Court and pays his fine just like anyone else." Imagine! Pays his $2 fines just like anyone else!

"He's a role model for adults and kids," Hardekopf goes on, possibly quoting Mister Falk or the ad copy for *I Can't Accept Not Trying*. "The great part of the story is that here is a guy who doesn't need the money, and whether he makes it or not in baseball, he pursued his dream—and perhaps because of him, more people will be willing to pursue their dreams."

But Hardekopf comes to the real point with *USA Today*. "We sold more merchandise in the first month he was here than we did in the first eight months of last year . . . We think Michael will do for us what *Bull Durham* did for the Durham Bulls. Durham is still one of the most popular minor-league teams. We think we'll have a national presence for years to come because of Michael. He'll still be helping us long after he's gone."

Diamond Dig

Friday night, June 10, is Diamond Dig Night at Historic Engel Stadium in Chattanooga. After the Barons-Lookouts double-header, the women in the crowd will be invited down on the field to search for a buried $2,700 diamond ring.

Michael looks so lame at the plate this evening that unsympathetic fans are yelling things like, "Underhand it to him!" and "Put it on a tee!" But he's up there hacking, and lo and behold, he connects. In most Southern League parks he'd have his first dinger, but in spacious Engel Stadium it merely bounces over the fence at the WUSY 101 sign in left center for a ground-rule double. But still!

After the second game, as he jets to Chicago to appear at the Michael Jordan/Ronald McDonald charity golf tournament tomorrow, four hundred women crawl around in the infield dirt, digging with plastic spoons for the buried diamond ring.

No ring. Lookouts personnel join the hunt. The grounds crew eventually brings picks, rakes, shovels, and metal-detectors. Who knows? The ring was buried this afternoon and apparently dislodged when the grounds crew dragged the infield. Or was buried too deep in the first place. Finally the Lookouts pick a winner out of a hat. She can pick up a duplicate at the jeweler's tomorrow.

Saturday's *Free Press* reports that Lookouts people stayed out there searching until 4 A.M. In vain.

———

Saturday's sports section also reports, in its "On This Date" box, that one year ago today "Michael Jordan and Charles Barkley each scored 42 points as the Chicago Bulls downed the Phoenix Suns for a 2–0 series lead in the NBA Finals."

ROOKIE

But if Michael has been less successful this year, he follows up last night's long double with some more encouraging work. Having jetted back from Chicago after a few hours on the golf course, he lines a two-run single in the sixth inning and triples into the right-field corner in the ninth to climb to .205. Lookouts manager Pat Kelly says, "He shows a lot more bat speed than a month and a half ago. He's made tremendous strides. The hits he got in this series were balls he hit hard. That wasn't the case in April."

———

I finally hear from a guy named Pat O'Conner of the National Association of Professional Baseball Leagues, Inc.—the Minor Leagues. My written complaint to the minor-league offices in St. Petersburg was forwarded to him, and Mr. O'Conner has looked into the situation.

"Based on the nature of [my] project," his fax says, he finds the Barons "to be justified in their stance on [my] credentials." He mentions "the need to protect the sanctity of the Barons' clubhouse" and how "intrusions into that area . . . can adversely affect the players."

I'm wondering how the sanctity of the Barons' clubhouse is maintained when Shaquille O'Neal drops in, or Charles Barkley and Cornelius Bennett and "about ten of their closest, most raucous friends."

Obviously, I was the villain in the story Mr. O'Conner got from the Barons. At the end of his fax he gently but unmistakably slaps me by suggesting I work *with* the Barons (his emphasis) in an effort to complete my project.

Still, it sounds as if I'll get somewhere if I'm willing to make nice.

———

Diamond Dig

In the press box at Bill Meyer Stadium in Knoxville (named for the Knoxville native who managed the Pittsburgh Pirates from 1948 to 1952 and was National League Manager of the Year in 1948), I humble myself and approach Chris Pika, who's feeding on chips and Old El Paso Jalapeño Cheese Sauce. "How are you, Chris? Look, I talked to a man in the minor-league office who suggested I work *with* you guys on my project."

Apparently afraid someone might cut in on the cheese sauce, Pika scarcely looks up. *Unh-unh. You're working for yourself; your book is unauthorized; Michael is an unwilling subject.* I'll get zippo from the Barons, no matter what the man said.

The potentate reigns.

The Heroes Have
Left the Building

"You show me a capitalist, I'll show you a bloodsucker."
— Malcolm X, *Malcolm X Speaks*

A couple of days after an unknown assailant brutally murders O. J. Simpson's wife and a friend, *USA Today* runs a half-page ad for *I Can't Accept Not Trying* under a headline asking, "What Makes an American Hero?" ("In his life and in his latest book, Michael Jordan shows us all that we can achieve great things if we only try. An American hero, Michael Jordan is an inspiration to us all.")

Meanwhile, we're witnessing the probable fall of another "American hero," O. J., who used to be Michael-with-a-football and probably could have scored with his own book of homilies twenty years ago.

Various commentators point out that O. J. was a sports hero, not an American hero, and that we'll go on being confounded until we start making the distinction.

It's a bad summer for sports stars. Diego Maradona, the world's greatest soccer player not long ago, is suspended yet again for having unacceptable substances in his body, this time during the World Cup. The same week, Dwight "Doctor K" Gooden, once baseball's greatest pitcher, is suspended for flunking a drug test—not a first for Doc, either. Darryl Straw-

The Heroes Have Left the Building

berry, once "the next Willie Mays," is trying to come back from his latest suspension. Jennifer Capriati, once one of tennis's great hopes, gets busted at a motel in Florida. John Daly's in trouble with golf officials again. Mickey Mantle is fresh out of the Betty Ford Clinic. Mike Tyson is still pleading innocent from the penitentiary.

Do we need any more proof, at this late date, that athletic prowess doesn't translate into noble character any more than, for instance, noble character translates into athletic prowess?

———

Yet there's always been something irresistible about the triumphant athlete. Even Red Smith, the legendary sports columnist, admitted he was occasionally guilty of "godding up the ballplayers." In Arthur Miller's *Death of a Salesman*, broken-down Willy Loman clings to his son Biff's long-ago high-school football glory: "Like a young god. Hercules—something like that. And the sun, the sun all around him. Remember how he waved to me? . . . and the cheers when he came out—Loman! Loman! Loman! God Almighty . . . A star like that, magnificent, can never really fade away."

Biff Loman had long since faded away, but Arthur Miller understood the inclination to idealize even small-time sports heroes. Michael Jordan, of course, passed into god territory back around 1992.

His life became unreal. Money hadn't been a concern since his first pro contract, but by now all doors were open to him. The rich and famous and powerful knelt before him; he was like royalty. *Ah, Michael! Yes, Michael. Right away, Mr. Jordan* . . .

In *The Frenzy of Renown: Fame and Its History*, Leo Brady writes, "The celebrity is constantly being told how great he is

ROOKIE

by a phalanx of yes-men and supporters, so his sense of self-justification is so much stronger."

That is, once you believe you're truly wonderful, truly a cut above "normal people," then you give your actions any name you want. If you're O.J., 911 episodes become marital "spats." If you're greedy and power-mad . . . well, *your* pursuit of riches isn't greed; it's something understandable and acceptable and probably even admirable, even if you can't think of the word. Power hungry? You just like to "be in control," which is something different.

Oddly, people buy it. People do want heroes. And there are millions, to this day, who not only ascribe admirable qualities to top athletes (which they wouldn't dream of doing with top artists, writers, ballet dancers, or mathemeticians), but ascribe them in amounts roughly corresponding to the player's stature in the sports world. Michael was hyped as not only the toughest, fiercest, most maniacally competitive of all, but at the same time as the sweetest, humblest, cuddliest, most generous, and most profound of all, joyously competing with healthy kids on playgrounds for a bottle of juice and beaming his smile down on sick kids in hospital beds (and making them well).

Through the wonders of hype, it sticks. And nothing else sticks, nothing that mars the pretty picture. We always sort of knew that Michael had to be obsessive to achieve what he did in basketball, and couldn't be other than self-absorbed, given the nonstop MichaelMichaelMichaelness of his life—but we didn't want to stop and think about it. We preferred the Michael we imagined, the Michael we wanted him to be.

We always sort of knew he was as lusty for money as for NBA championships, and if we knew anything about Mister Falk, we knew the pursuit wasn't always pretty—but we didn't give it much thought.

The Heroes Have Left the Building

We overlooked the disenchantment of his Bulls teammates in Sam Smith's *The Jordan Rules*. Michael bashed Smith ("The book was at odds with The Image," Smith says) even though, revealingly, he never challenged the book's accuracy and his teammates never backed off their unflattering statements.

We shrugged off Michael's low-life associations and never mentioned his shamelessness in writing them off as "goons" when the associations became public and threatened his pre-eminence as a pitchman. Shameless? Michael? Couldn't be.

He'll probably never wind up like O.J., but he's got his warps. The picture has certainly changed for me since I got smacked in the face with proof that either Michael or the fellow who's directed his affairs for the last ten years is staggeringly, breathtakingly greedy. Or both of them.

The pretty picture has clouded. That stuff I never wanted to think about has come into focus.

———

Mister Falk is the man behind the empire. He's been with Michael since the twenty-one-year-old came out of the University of North Carolina in 1984. Mister Falk will tell you, naturally, that he's doing all the things he does *for Michael*, but of course there was a time when he didn't even know Michael Jordan and there was only one reason to get acquainted— namely, the possibility of money to be made for Mister Falk.

But if Mister Falk is the last person on earth I'd call a role model, he's got his own tidy self-justifications. He's been known to talk about the numbers of people who despise him as a sort of merit badge. "There are people who don't like me because I'm very opinionated, but I think they respect me. I'd like to be liked *and* respected, but sometimes there are trade-offs. I would rather be respected than liked. The nature of what

ROOKIE

I do—taking money, getting more money—they are not likely to like you."

Convenient. But lots of opinionated people, as well as money-people, are not only liked but also respected *as human beings*. Mister Falk's line is true to a point—he *is* respected—but he ignores the distinction others make: he's respected as a moneymaker and power broker, and *that's all*. "You'll find a grudging admiration for the man," Jack McCallum allowed in a *Sports Illustrated* profile. "But there is certainly no rush to break bread with him."

"He's a shark," says *Jordan Rules* author Sam Smith. "Very persuasive, very tough negotiator—very successful. Personally? When David needs you, he talks to you. When he doesn't, he doesn't."

"He's honest by the rules of his game," says writer Jeff Coplon. "But those rules are fast and loose."

Indeed, for what it's worth, Falk's ethics may be no more elastic than those of most other agents. But then, even agents will tell you there's no handbook for the job, no rules that *must* be followed except "Stop short of criminal conduct, for your own good"—and, as we know, people in all walks of life work around that one every day.

But whatever his methods, whatever his personality, Mister Falk had a big hand in making Michael filthy rich. He got him an unprecedented sneaker deal as soon as Michael entered the NBA—not just the usual contract to wear the shoes and make a few ads, but his own shoe line. By wearing Nike apparel at the slam-dunk contest during his rookie season, Michael became the first player to blatantly commercialize such an event. And Nike was just the beginning. The Air Jordan ads made Michael bigger than life, and by the early 1990s Mister Falk had used the power of the image to turn Michael into a ubiquitous pitchman.

The Heroes Have Left the Building

The product didn't seem to matter much. McDonald's, Wheaties, Nike, and more. Watches, greeting cards, cars, clothes, lottery tickets. Nike's Phil Knight offered the opinion that Michael cheapened his image by advertising underwear (Hanes)—but at least he did actual commercials for Hanes. "One of the vehicles I've pursued over the last three years," Mister Falk was quoted in Jim Naughton's *Taking to the Air: The Rise of Michael Jordan*, "is to become more aggressive on the marketing side, passively using [Michael's] name to sell sleeping bags, trading cards, golf equipment, back-to-school notebooks, lunch pails, whatever" . . .

Whatever.

. . . "as opposed to making eight or ten appearances a year for Coca-Cola bottlers or McDonald's franchise operators."

Almost anything legal, it seemed. Donald Katz writes in his recent book *Just Do It: The Nike Spirit in the Corporate World*, "Falk didn't just talk about a deal and let it sit. He liked to be part of the creative process. He'd throw out ideas fast and furiously, wave his arms, and say, 'Hey, you don't like that one? No? Well, here's another one.' "

Even before the Bulls won their first NBA championship in 1991, Michael's fame had started building upon itself, growing exponentially with every season of ads and exposure. But it was *over*exposure, *over*hype—overkill. By the time the Bulls broke through to take the title in 1991, the backlash was beginning in some quarters. A few months later New York columnist Mike Lupica wrote, "The truth is, if I could be like Mike . . . I think I'd try to be a little more invisible. Nike. Gatorade. McDonald's. Hanes. The Michael Jordan television special. *Saturday Night Live*. That hype started to get a little tiresome last spring during the NBA finals. Good grief. Jordan wasn't just a great player trying to win his first pro championship.

ROOKIE

That wasn't big enough for NBC. Instead they had to make it a religious experience.

"If Chicago didn't get the NBA title, there was no reason for any of us to go on. When the NBC cameras finally found him, kissing the trophy in the locker room after the Bulls had defeated the Lakers, we were presented with a bigger tear-jerker than the parting scene in *E.T.* Air Grail had finally won."

Tom Callahan wrote in the *Washington Post*, "Beyond much doubt now, Michael Jordan is the finest athlete and most tire-some person in the country."

But Mister Falk, lining his pockets, was one happy fellow. And Michael, all evidence indicates, was one more.

It was in the year of the second championship, 1992, that Michael fully transformed from mere superstar to full-fledged comic-book superhero. The $40 million a year for endorse-ments, the second NBA title, the Dream Team that summer. Michael was all-powerful, going so far as challenging the U.S. Olympic Committee on its promise the players would wear Reebok apparel on the medal stand.

"I feel very strongly about my loyalty to my shoe company," Michael said—to which Baltimore columnist Mike Littwin riposted, "I'm waiting for him to say he regrets he has but one life to give to his shoe company."

Los Angeles scribe Scott Ostler chimed in, "Jordan, I hear, really wanted to take part in the opening ceremonies but backed out when the USOC denied him permission to wear a huge Nike shoe on his head."

After months of debasing public dialogue, the Dream Team did wear Reebok, but Michael had won the right to cover up all traces of Nike's competitor on the medal stand by draping himself in an American flag. If he compromised spontaneity, he underscored his conviction that's he's got the right to make every penny he can and concede nothing, if possible.

The Heroes Have Left the Building

According to Katz's *Just Do It*, Phil Knight and even Michael wondered whether the hype had gone too far, but neither one wanted to stop it or even take responsibility for it. Knight said, "Do I think Nike creates images for athletes that exceed their capacity to perform as athletes—or as real people? Well, my short answer is yes, but it's not just us. It's TV that really defines these athletes. We just expand on the image. But perhaps our efforts do combine with the power of television to come together and create something that nobody can live up to."

Perhaps.

Certainly Mister Falk wouldn't pull the plug. As arrogant and grandiose as he is, he's remained sufficiently grounded in reality to concede, "Having Michael has brought me my identity, and it would be silly to deny it. I can call up the CEO of any company in the United States, and if they don't know my name, they'll still take my call when they find out I represent Michael Jordan."

It's a heady feeling. "I enjoy being in the flow," Mister Falk has said. "You want to feel a little bit like a power broker."

Even if your power stems solely from your association with a certain client, and could vanish at that client's whim. "I think Michael is in a position [where], if he wanted to, he could leverage our company and me to do almost anything he wanted. And you ask yourself, would you risk losing a client of his importance? How high would you jump if he cracked the whip?"

His own man, Mister Falk is.

Even as Michael kept getting bigger and bigger, richer and richer, he was increasingly unhappy by some accounts. Donald Katz, interviewed prior to the publication of *Just Do It* in 1994, said, "As the book goes on, as Michael Jordan's psychic state becomes more and more tenuous, you feel the people at Nike

ROOKIE

know they have been part of a process that has not been good for this young man."

Michael had gotten too big. He couldn't go out in public without being swarmed. He registered in hotels under assumed names. Friends had to meet him secretly in hotel suites. He could hardly trust anyone—almost everyone he met wanted something from him, even if only the ego-gratification of his company. He told *Sports Illustrated*'s Jack McCallum, "I look forward to playing now more than ever. It's the only place I can get relief from what's happening off the court."

Certainly, he saw as little as ever of his wife and his three young children.

He had long ago bought into that life, of course, but he shamelessly played on it in the Nike ad that aired during the 1993 NBA finals. We saw Michael alone in a dimly lit gym, shooting free throws, nothing but Michael and the bounce and swish and bounce and swish of the ball . . . and heard Michael's sober voice-over, "What if my name wasn't in lights? What if my face wasn't on TV every other second? What if there wasn't a crowd around every corner? What if I was just a basketball player? Can you imagine it? I can."

But it could never happen, of course; he was long past that. And we "normal people," watching the ad, wanted to scream, *You* could *have been just a basketball player!* You *(and Mister Falk) put yourself on TV every other second! You sold out a long time ago; don't cry about it now! Don't blame your adoring public!*

He was losing it. During the 1993 finals, one of his California cronies self-published a book claiming Michael had lost more than a million dollars to him on the golf course. After the press made much of Michael's trip to Atlantic City with his father the night before a game, Michael refused to speak to reporters for a week or so. He broke his silence, finally, with an

The Heroes Have Left the Building

interview by his buddy, NBC lightweight Ahmad Rashad—for which Michael inexplicably wore shades, as if he wanted to look bad even while reassuring us of his virtue. Even NBA commissioner David Stern, interviewed by Bob Costas, was reduced to stammers in trying to gloss over the whole business.

The spell was broken, somehow, even as Michael led the Bulls to their third straight championship. Who could fail to see the ironies in that Nike spot? Michael, who had bought into the whole scheme that made him larger than life and mind-bogglingly rich, now played the poor-pitiful-me card—in another *ad*, the point of which was to burn him even deeper into our brains. You could almost picture Michael in the boardroom with all the blow-dried pinky-ring types, thinking, *Yeah, that'll work. People will feel for me. They should, with all I endure simply for being great and being a role model.*

We didn't expect him to retire a few months later. When he did, he talked about spending more time with his wife and kids—"watching the grass grow, and then cutting it"—but that didn't sound like Michael. When Mister Falk assured us Michael was a well-rounded individual capable of much more than playing basketball, we anticipated a symphony or a novel or a run for office.

It turned out that Michael had been disingenuous about spending more time with his family—that is, he'd lied. He had already told White Sox owner Jerry Reinsdorf he wanted to try baseball. He would work on his hitting in Chicago all winter, take off for spring training in February, and, if all went well, spend the summer traveling around playing ball.

And so it came to pass. And if many people were good and tired of MichaelMichaelMichael by then, there were still plenty of idolators. People with a need to believe.

Nike knew it. Michael knew it too well. There he was, his

earnest face filling the TV screen this past spring as he asked us, "What if there were no more sports? Would I still be your hero?"

Still?

You couldn't help thinking the young man was gone on himself.

———

Image versus reality.

I get hold of one of my brother-in-law's friends in Chattanooga, the owner of the limousine service NBC hired for Tom Brokaw's *Now* piece back in April.

"NBC News called on a Wednesday," as he recollects, "and booked a limo for Tom Brokaw and his crew on Saturday. Brokaw was on his way to Egypt but he was going to stop and do this interview with Jordan. Friday NBC called back saying they needed a car for Michael Jordan on Saturday, too, to get him to the stadium for the interview and back to the hotel. We were booked for Saturday, but I have a Lincoln Town Car of my own and I told 'em I'd take him myself. I thought it might be kind of fun.

"Saturday, one driver picks up Brokaw and his people and takes 'em to the stadium. They're as nice as can be. Meanwhile, I go to the Holiday Inn to pick up Jordan at 1:30. He and his golfing buddy don't show up until 2:15—which I don't mind, because NBC hired the car for the afternoon, but my other driver is calling and saying Brokaw's in a hurry, where's Jordan?

"So Jordan gets in my car with four buddies from the team. It's a fifteen-minute ride to the stadium, and all the way it was, 'M——f—— this, m——f—— that.' They were talking about a club they'd been to the night before and Jordan was telling these young guys, 'Did you see those babes last night, they were all over me, I could've had anything I wanted,' all this.

The Heroes Have Left the Building

"I took my own car out on my afternoon off because I thought it might be kind of fun, but it was a waste of time. He wasn't what you see on TV."

Just your basic guy, more or less, talking like lots of guys talk a lot of the time. Nothing criminal in it. In fact, the conversation showed Michael resisting (as other basketball superstars have not) the temptations that all mortals feel. The point being that Michael *is* a mere mortal, a regular guy more or less— even if he's got some of the obsession and self-absorption that's inevitable in his kind of genius, and by now has been warped by too much money and too much adulation and too much association with the likes of Mister Falk.

We wouldn't be so disappointed to find him as coarse as the rest of us . . . if only he and Mister Falk and the advertisers didn't continuously hold him up as something better.

———

In late June, league president Jimmy Bragan extends Michael an invitation to play in the Double-A All-Star Game in Binghamton, New York on July 11, citing the Southern League's thirty percent jump in paying customers this season. "I told him, 'The game's already a sellout, so you won't be there to sell tickets. With the influence you've had on Southern League attendance, you've earned it.' And he had."

Michael—third from the bottom among Southern League hitters, leading all outfielders in errors, a very mediocre 20-for-32 in stolen bases—has the grace to decline.

"He told me he wanted to talk it over with his wife," Bragan says, "and I think she vetoed it. He said he wanted to spend some time with his wife and children. That was good enough for me.

"I guess when you're making 30 or 40 million dollars a year, your time is more important than that."

Dog Days

"He that would have the fruit must climb the tree."

— Thomas Fuller, *Gnomologia*

Reports out of Chicago saying Michael is about to give up baseball and rejoin the Bulls this fall are immediately quashed. Terry Francona tells reporters, "The only indication I get is that he's enjoying the heck out of himself and wants to make it to the major leagues."

Bulls GM Jerry Krause says, "Fans should get used to the idea that Michael Jordan is not going to be back with this team. We do want to see Michael in a Chicago uniform—a White Sox uniform."

And though Michael continues to struggle, White Sox GM Ron Schueler says the club hasn't given up on him. "Not yet, as long as he doesn't give up. I think a couple of times, mentally, he has been down. But he fought back and right now his attitude is real good."

Michael quiets the speculation about a return to the NBA by telling reporters in Birmingham, "I don't like to close doors, but if you want me to say it, OK: never. I will never play basketball again, except recreationally." He admits he considered quitting baseball a month ago but was reassured by Francona and the Barons' coaches. "They told me I had made good progress and the potential was there. It was encouraging.

Dog Days

"Nothing has changed since the end of spring training. We said we would look at things at the end of the season and make a decision then. The end of the season is not here yet."

———

The crowds keep coming. By July 3 Michael is floundering at .193, but the Barons draw 12,625 to Hoover Stadium for the game against Nashville and fireworks afterward—the biggest crowd of the season, the biggest since 13,279 attended the first game in the park back in 1988. Michael (his pants disappearing into his hightops once again, no more Negro League look) manages an infield single and scores a run in the Barons' 3–2 win over the Xpress.

On July 4, the forty-third home date of the season, the crowd of 9,158 pushes the Barons' attendance over last season's total for sixty-seven games. They're averaging 6,600 at home, 8,600 on the road.

A ground-ball single off the shortstop's glove gives Michael another 1-for-4 in the Barons' 8–0 stomping of the Xpress, and he's up to .195.

Wednesday night's game with Huntsville brings one of the highlights of Michael's season so far. It wouldn't seem like much—it's not even a base hit—but Michael says so himself later.

The Barons, trailing 5–0 going into the bottom of the ninth, make it 5–3 by the time Michael steps up with the bases loaded and two outs. The PA system plays the Alan Parsons Project's "Sirius," the throbbing synthesizer piece the Bulls used to play during those dramatic lights-out, spotlit introductions in Chicago Stadium. After a check-swing strike and a weak foul for strike two, down to the Barons' last gasp, Michael hits a sharp one-hopper to the Stars' third baseman—who bobbles it, then cuts loose a hurried throw over the first baseman's head. All three runners score; Barons win, 6–5; Michael "knocks in" the winning runs!

"When I heard that music from Chicago Stadium," he says afterward, "I got pimples all over my arms. It seemed like basketball all over again."

As far as working the count against the Huntsville pitcher in the ninth, "I think that's where my experience in basketball helped out. I was calm in that situation and just let my abilities come out—what little abilities I have . . . That's the best feeling I've had since I started playing this game. I was not a gimmick. I was not a sideshow. I was part of this team and I helped us win. That's what I've always thrived on."

———

On July 13, the day after the major-league All-Star Game, I head up the Great Smoky Mountains Expressway to catch up with Michael and the Barons in Knoxville. Sooty low-hanging clouds and the ominous smell in the air promise more thunderstorms as I head into Great Smoky Mountains National Park and the tourist town of Cherokee.

Cherokee, the old Indian reservation, is a beautiful place for the most part, with its stately old hardwood trees and quiet little river and the Museum of the Cherokee Indian. But the center of town is the tackiest place you can imagine: a long, bustling strip of shops with names like "Trading Post" that deal in cheesy, cheapo, faux-Indian moccasins, pottery, crafts, masks. Everything's in an Indian motif except, of course, the Burger King and Baskin-Robbins and Kentucky Fried Chicken that find their way into every tourist town.

Pigeon Forge is next, and just as tacky: a stretch of motels and amusements and rides and factory outlets; a little Elvis

Dog Days

museum, Forbidden Caverns, helicopter rides, Smoky Mountains this-and-that . . .

———

In Knoxville, Michael's return is scarcely mentioned in the *News-Sentinel*. After all, it's mid-July, less than two months until college football starts, and here in Big Orange country (Knoxville's the home of the University of Tennessee Volunteers) baseball might as well not exist. Even with the world's most famous athlete in town for the last time this season, Gary Lundy's sports column is a lighthearted look at SEC football coaches.

I sit in the press box with beat writer Bob Hodge, a good ol' Tennessee boy whose response when an out-of-towner asks about Knoxville is that, uh, it's pretty dull until football season. Chewing Skoal and spitting into a pop bottle, he tells me, "During football season I cover a high-school game every Friday night. On Saturday I go to the UT game if it's at home; if it's on the road, my friends and I play football, then watch on TV. On Sunday I go to the sports bar and watch the Minnesota Vikings, my team, and then watch the Sunday night game. And then there's always the Monday night game."

And Bob Hodge is by no means an atypical Tennessean—or Southerner, for that matter.

The fans at Bill Meyer Stadium still react when Michael, accompanied by seven cops, appears for warm-ups—they clap and yell more than they do for the other players—but they don't go nuts or try to get down close. It's more or less another night at the park. Still, Michael's escort is right with him as he leaves the field for the last few minutes before the game starts, apparently protecting him from Smokies mascot Alfredo the Owl and WIVC radio's Wivic the Frog.

ROOKIE

"That offends me," Bob Hodge says, and spits into the pop bottle.

"Alfredo? Wivic the Frog?"

"Seven cops offend me. Knoxville has too many problems to have seven cops escorting this schmuck." He points to the neighborhoods beyond the left–center-field fence. "There are people over there probably getting beat up right now—people who *need* cops."

Michael, coming into the series at .194, is still trying to get comfortable at the plate. He's choking up on the bat an inch or so, the first time I've seen that, and he's opened up his stance a little, his front (left) foot pulled back a few inches from the plate.

In the third inning he takes a strike, then lines a breaking ball up the middle for a single—a line drive, but hardly a scorcher. Still working on that bat speed.

Next time up, he goes after the first pitch and grounds out to third. Third time, he again attacks the first pitch and grounds to shortstop.

After walking down to a concession stand for a hot dog, I pause to watch from the lower level and wind up talking to a guy in the stands who happened to comment on my Portland, Oregon T-shirt. He turns out to be a pitcher, Kyle Dewey, twenty-six years old, who's just been released by the Smokies. He's sitting with his roommates: one of the Smokies' starting pitchers (who's charting pitches tonight) and his girlfriend.

"I'm not upset about getting cut," Dewey insists, though the baseball future isn't bright for a twenty-six-year-old who got bombed in Triple A last season and compiled a 4.28 ERA here this year. "I've been getting screwed around and this will give me a chance to catch on somewhere where I'll get a fair chance. Our rent is paid through the end of the month, so there's no hurry."

Dog Days

Michael? Kyle Dewey chuckles. "I faced him twice earlier this season—got him to ground out and strike out. You jam him, because he's got long arms, and throw breaking balls away. You can jam him all day."

In the Smokies' locker room after the game, Bob Hodge and I hear the same thing from Aaron Small, the young pitcher who got a glare from Michael tonight after hitting him with a pitch. "I pitched against him in spring training, and you just try to give him fastballs in and breaking balls away. He got two hits off me earlier this year and they were both on fastballs away. Tonight I wanted to make sure I got my fastball inside. The pitch I hit him with was one that ran in on him a little too much." Michael actually took a few angry steps toward Small. "I couldn't believe he was mad. Like I was *trying* to hit him."

As Bob Hodge questions a kid named Bowers who knocked in the winning run, I keep thinking I'm seeing former major leaguer Bill Buckner across the room. It looks a little like him—the face, the thick mustache—but this guy is so small, and so youthful, and why would Bill Buckner be here anyway, wearing a Knoxville uniform? The last I heard, he was not only out of baseball but had moved his family to Idaho or somewhere to escape legions of New Englanders who continued to blame his infamous muff for the defeat of the Boston Red Sox in the 1986 World Series.

But a few minutes later, seeing a little kid in a "BUCKNER 14" jersey hanging around the trim fellow's locker—Buckner's son, obviously—I walk over and introduce myself to a guy who batted .289 while collecting 2,715 major-league hits between 1971 and 1990.

Turns out Buckner's working for the Toronto Blue Jays, the Smokies' parent club, as a roving hitting instructor.

His thoughts on Michael?

ROOKIE

"When I heard he was going to give baseball a shot I was impressed with his commitment and his willingness to work. But it's difficult to come in and play baseball like that after so long . . . to the point where, to me, he's done a pretty good job to be hitting .198. He's a great athlete, and I'm sure he would have been a very good baseball player if he had made it his career, but . . ."

Buckner doesn't see any insurmountable horrors in Michael's swing. "He's a big guy and he's gotta generate a little bit more power . . . which will come, but you've gotta take a lot of swings to do that. You've got to get your mechanics right to where you use your legs, hips, and upper body to generate some bat speed. He's getting it, but baseball is a lot of instinct, and you develop those instincts by playing. He was very raw early in the year and he's come around a lot, but it's gonna take another year of Double A and . . . He just needs time. He's got a chance to make the major leagues, but I'd say he needs at least a thousand more at-bats—winter ball, more minor-league ball. It depends on what kind of commitment he wants to make."

In the manager's office down the hall I find the Smokies' thirty-five-year-old boss, Garth Iorg, a .258 hitter in nine years with the Blue Jays.

"I think what Jordan is doing is great," says the affable Iorg. "I think it's great that he's willing to try something different. And he really has shocked me with what he's done so far. I'm a fan."

Iorg believes Michael would have been a great ballplayer had the other game not sidetracked him back in high school. "With his size and leverage, and learning how to hit when he was eighteen years old, yeah, he'd be hittin' some *bombs*. You take Dave Kingman [442 home runs in the majors], who had a similar body . . . Dave Winfield [463 and counting] . . . Michael would be in their class. He'd be hittin' *bombs*."

Dog Days

How does Michael, who has been striking out much less often, make the jump from simply hitting the ball to hitting it hard? How does he turn those tepid line drives into screamers?

"Time. Nothing but time, and I don't know how much time he has. We get guys at eighteen years old, and every year the better ones grow by leaps and bounds. I think Jordan's got a *good* swing, and if he maintains his improvement . . . But again, it's a question of whether he has enough time, agewise, before he starts getting diminishing returns on his talent."

Iorg isn't convinced Michael should play winter ball. "I think he needs some time away from it, to soak in what he's learned. I know that in my career, when I went away from it for a while, all that coaching seemed to come together naturally. It's like golf: you're out there every day hackin', hackin', fightin' this and that, and then you go away for a while and when you come back it's like, 'OK, yeah, *that's* what they meant!' "

Iorg, like Buckner, thinks people don't give Michael credit for what he's accomplished, considering the circumstances. I'm reminded that *I* thought he'd flunk out in spring training; I would have been surprised to hear that in mid-July he'd be hovering around .200 in Double A and only striking out (recently) about a quarter of the time.

"Anyone who knocks him," Iorg says, "doesn't know how tough it is. Aaron Small, who pitched tonight, has pitched in the major leagues. Jose Silva [also on the Smokies] is going to pitch in the major leagues. A lot of these guys. The talent Michael is seeing day in and day out . . . when he looks back after he's finished, he's going to see a lot of these guys *starring* in the major leagues.

"Can he make it? Who knows? I wouldn't put any limitations on him, simply because of his talent and work ethic. Guys

ROOKIE

like him can overcome a lot in a short time. If you're talking
about a utility-type outfielder ... His arm from right field
would have to improve a little bit, but as far as running down
balls, he should be as good as anyone. The physical tools are all
there, if he has enough time."

The Struggle Continues

"With audacity one can undertake anything, but not do everything."

— Napoléon I, *Maxims*

After a five-day, 2-for-20 home stand drops Michael to .188, his lowest ebb yet, I follow the Barons down to Jacksonville. Down through picturesque Savannah; down through poor rural communities in south Georgia, with battered trailers and small run-down houses; down through little Woodbine, "Home of Georgia's Crawfish Festival," where you start seeing palm trees and Spanish moss.

On Fernandina Beach near Jacksonville, I'm feeling fortunate yet again to be an anonymous speck in the world, free to stroll down a beach and take it all in at my leisure: black and white; young and old; families, singles, lovers . . . swimming, fishing, walking, lying in the sand; guy-gal sets of lifeguards perched on elevated chairs every so often; gentle dunes beyond them, with seaoats swaying in the sea breeze; and beyond the dunes, the long stretch of bungalows and cottages and condos, with people lolling on the porches and taking in the scene themselves. It's heaven, even when the rumbling purple clouds in the distance suddenly move in as if on a jet stream and the beach clears in a matter of minutes.

I sit in my car reading the *Florida Times-Union* as lightning

ROOKIE

flashes over the ocean and the deluge dins on the roof. The headline on the sports page indicates Michael's return is no big deal: "No longer a hot ticket," with the subhead "Jordan's appeal sinks with batting average." Nonetheless, it *is* the headline, and almost all of page one is Michael: the first half of the lead story, the first half of a column, a big color picture, and a chart ("Deflating Air") showing Michael's ebbing fortunes since his early-season mini-streak. On page two, in agate type, they've got Michael's game-by-game lines from day one: date, at-bats, runs, hits, RBI, batting average.

Reading Tony Fabrizio's column, I'm struck again by Michael's concern about what people think of him. Up in Birmingham recently he told Fabrizio—who was sufficiently legitimate to get into the locker room—"When people see me here [in the minor leagues], hopefully they'll see that I love the game. I'm not trying to gain media hype. I'm not trying to get endorsements. It's just for the love of playing. I'm not making any great money doing this."

It's OK, Michael. We always believed you loved the game, and we understand that you enjoy athletic challenges and don't need more money in any case. Do your thing.

Michael also lets Fabrizio in on a little-known reason why he's enjoying his summer. "Every place I've been, I've had some great soul food. It's given me a great chance to catch up on Southern food because I've been in Chicago a long time."

———

I head out to Wolfson Park three hours before game time. Though the skies have cleared, stretches of the roads around the park are a foot deep in water. All you can do is back up and look for another road, but you just keep running into more water.

The Struggle Continues

Returning near game time from another direction, I find a viable street and a parking attendant who directs me past the packed lots into a marshy field, where I'm slipping and skidding in six inches of muck and wondering whether, if I do get safely in, I'll be able to get out later.

Tonight at Wolfson Park: Homer Hankies to the first 2,000 women, sponsored by Community First Bank and Fox TV 30, WAWS. Also, sponsored by Bacardi, ladies twenty-one and over can buy general-admission tickets for a dollar and Breezers (a Bacardi drink) for a dollar.

And Michael Jordan. The fans, who know by now they're not seeing history, aren't giddy like they were the first time, but they're here—8,063 of them compared to the Suns' average crowd of 3,681.

The game is uneventful except for a moment in the second inning when, with the Barons in the field, two young dolts who've probably had too many Breezers jump the fence down the right-field line and trot out to Michael, the drowsy cops in belated pursuit. Michael's got to be a little alarmed, but once they arrive he realizes they're harmless; he shakes one's hand, and they exchange a few words before the cops get there. The pair depart the field triumphantly, grinning and clasping hands overhead like a victorious tag team even as an old cop gently twists one's free arm behind his back. Back outside the fence they get a brief talking-to, then they're ejected from the park. But you know it's worth it to them: they're the type who'll brag about this caper for the rest of their lives, and their friends are the type who'll be impressed.

Michael seems to have closed his stance again, moving his front foot nearer to the plate, but he's still uncertain, still flailing as he goes 0-for-2 with a hit-by-pitch.

Mike Barnett swears that Michael's getting better. All the

baseball men do, and it stands to reason he would be, but improvement in baseball sometimes comes in such tiny increments that it might be next year before anyone but baseball men can see it.

———

After Michael totals 1-for-7 the next two nights, I'm back on the road, headed for my sister's place in Palm Harbor on the Gulf Coast.

I pull up at Becky and Bob's house at 7 A.M. Even at this hour, the heavy tropical air is alive with birds singing shrill, bizarre songs; geckoes skitter out of range as I come up the sidewalk; scents change every few steps as I brush past hibiscus and oleander bushes, duck under lemon and fig and papaya and Mineola-orange branches.

By ten it's so steamy that when I come out of the air-conditioned house, my sunglasses fog up as soon as I open the front door.

It's a lifestyle. As Bob's van cruises down their street toward the marina, neighbors out in their yards seem, without fail, to have cold beer within reach. They raise cans in greeting as we pass, offering us our own if Bob so much as slows down to say hello. "How 'bout a cold beer?" "Can I buy y'a cold one?" "That calls for a cold one." "It's five o'clock somewhere. Can I buy ya one?"

After a day out in the boat, it's rumrunners at Crabby Bill's ("Don't worry, be crabby," Bill's T-shirts say); daiquiris at a place on the beach where everyone cheers and proposes toasts the instant someone determines the sun has officially set; and finally a dinner from the grill in the backyard and late-night talk on the screen porch, as fireflies blink outside and the infernal no-see-ums inflict minor torment. "No screen can

The Struggle Continues

keep 'em out," Bob says. "A no-see-um is nothing but a big mouth with wings."

———

Sunday's *Chicago Tribune* runs a long front-page Michael piece by staff writer Melissa Isaacson—who, as an employee of a legitimate news organization, had no trouble getting access in Birmingham.

Asked how he's coping with his father's murder at this point, Michael reveals that he broke down recently while watching a Wesley Snipes movie in his hotel room. "At the end his father died. The room was dark and I was lying on the bed and I guess it hit the right buttons because all of a sudden I couldn't stop crying. I talked to my wife. I called everyone I knew. And I still couldn't stop crying. I never had a day in my life that I felt that sad."

The two young delinquents charged with James Jordan's murder will go on trial this fall, but Michael says he won't attend. "The damage has been done. Justice may prevail, but there's no justice when there's no life."

Isaacson elicits more of Michael's outsized concern about what people think. He's been invited to play in Scottie Pippen's charity basketball game in Chicago Stadium on September 9—the last game to be played at the scene of Michael's greatest glories, with the Bulls moving into a new arena this fall—and he would love to take part, *but* "I couldn't play because people just don't want to let it die that I don't want to play organized basketball anymore. It would be great fun just to play it and not have people feeling that, hey, I miss the game so much I've got to come back and play.

"If I could just play and say, 'My career is over with, I don't want to play any more organized basketball, I just want to play

ROOKIE

these pickup games here and there' . . . it would be different. But I don't think that's possible."

Michael! *Michael!* It *is* possible, because as much as we'd all like to see you back doing your inimitable stuff, we're not losing sleep over it. Do what you want to do. Be M. J. the baseball player instead of M. J. the hoopster. The Beatles quit being Beatles and the earth kept turning; when people complained that they all made lesser music on their own, they said, *Up yours! We do what we please!*

"I would love to [play in Pippen's game]," Michael repeats. "I'm just so afraid"—*so afraid?*—"of the perception that I want to come back . . . I do miss the game; I just don't want to play it in uniforms and with referees and all that other stuff. What is so wrong with that?"

Nothing, Mike. Nobody's accusing you of anything. If you want to come back to the NBA, come on, but as Kevin McHale pointed out, they're going to play the season anyway. And our lives will go on.

———

They still come to see Michael in Orlando. An hour before the game, on the warning track behind home plate, batting coach Mike Barnett stands off at an angle underhanding balls to first baseman Troy Fryman, who whacks them into a screen straight ahead as a cluster of fans watches from the first row. These early arrivals have come down because, just behind Fryman, not twenty feet away from them, Michael leans on his black bat, waiting his turn.

When Fryman departs and Michael moves in and starts assaulting Barnett's lobs, the fans could almost reach out and touch him if not for the mesh backstop in between. As it is, they press against the mesh, dozens of them, taking pictures and shouting his name and, as people always do, simply gawking at him.

He takes a couple of dozen cuts. When he's finished, gathering up the balls and listening intently to a few words from Barnett, the mob is screeching, "Michael! Mike! Puh-*leeeze!*" One lady, who knows he's not going to come over and sign autographs, prods her little boy, "Louie, tell him 'Good job, Michael!' " and Louie dutifully shouts, "Good job, Michael!"

As Michael heads back to the third-base dugout, the bunch of kids moves over there, where they shout and reach out as he comes toward them, keeping it up even after he disappears into the dugout—while Michael, as usual, pretends not to hear. It's got to be weird.

Up in the press box I introduce myself to Peter Vecsey, the judge-jury-and-executioner *New York Post* basketball writer and NBC "NBA Insider." He says he takes summers off, mostly, but came down at his editor's request to do something on Michael. He's heard Michael does a press conference the first night in each town.

Only the first time around, I tell him, and Michael has done Orlando. But Vecsey isn't fazed. Vecsey's big, and Michael always talks to the big boys.

A season-high crowd of 6,742 jams little Tinker Field— "Beautiful Tinker Field," as the Cubs' PA man intones repeatedly, as in, "Tomorrow night's game at Beautiful Tinker Field starts at seven o'clock. Bring the kids out to Beautiful Tinker Field for the best entertainment value in town."

Michael looks hopeless in his first at-bat: takes a fastball for strike one, awkwardly check-swings on a change-up for strike two, and lunges after a curve for the whiff.

He's bailing out, his front foot moving towards third base as the pitch comes in. He seems to be standing closer to the plate than ever, apparently concerned about reaching the outside pitch, but he's so close he can hardly step into the ball without stepping on home plate. He's almost *got* to bail out, since any pitch on the inside part of the plate will look as if it's coming right at him.

Second time up, Michael bails again, then produces a lame foul pop-up to the first baseman.

In the seventh inning, he looks bad on a couple of strikes but then gets good wood on a line drive to center field—which takes off rising like a major-league shot, as if it's going over the center fielder's head, but then simply dies for an easy out. That's what Bill Buckner and Garth Iorg were talking about: if Michael ever gets his mechanics right, that ball is a *bomb*.

Most of the crowd departs Beautiful Tinker Field after Michael grounds into a double play in the top of the ninth, even though it looks as if there might be extra innings. As it turns out, Michael is instrumental in the Barons' winning rally in the thirteenth, laying down a bunt to move the go-ahead run into scoring position. Troy Fryman's double brings in the run and the Barons retire Orlando in the bottom of the thirteenth for the win.

———

Meanwhile, the cynics keep having fun with Michael's baseball fling. I make a rare purchase of *Baseball Weekly*, seeing the remarkable Frank Thomas ("Chasing History") on the cover, and find that Michael is part of the main feature, "The top ten races of the second half." You've got Frank Thomas vs. history, the Braves vs. the Expos, Donald Fehr and Richard Ravitch vs. the strike deadline, and so on—and a last one, "Michael Jordan vs. the Mendoza Line." There's a graph illustrating Michael's declining numbers, and *Baseball Weekly*'s forecast underneath: "Jordan will hit .205 and hit one home run."

The Struggle Continues

As far as Michael's prospects in Triple A (to say nothing of the majors) . . . as long as I've got a *Baseball Weekly*, I turn to the minor-league stats and look up Mike Robertson, the kid who lit up the Southern League for the Barons early in the season and earned a call-up to the Nashville Sounds. It turns out that the Double-A terror has been Jordanesque at the next level, hitting .190 in 147 at-bats. It's a tough game.

———

Still, the baseball men insist Michael is vastly improved. On Tuesday a roving batting instructor for the Chicago Cubs tells me it won't be long before Michael connects for a home run. As for the bigger picture, "There are three steps to hitting: getting set, reading the pitch, and firing. Michael is good at getting set and firing, but he doesn't always recognize pitches, so if he guesses wrong he's dead—he's already committed his swing to a certain spot. But he can learn that. He's getting better."

Rain cancels batting practice on Tuesday, so the overflow crowd of 6,421 at Beautiful Tinker Field doesn't see Michael until the Barons take the field for the bottom of the first inning. They roar as soon as he pops out of the dugout.

They go nuts when he lopes back in after three outs.

They cheer when he comes out to the on-deck circle moments later. They don't have long to watch him at bat, as Michael pops out to short center field on the second pitch, but they applaud appreciatively as he jogs back to the dugout. No cynicism here. Maybe Orlando has a soft spot for Michael from his NBA days. There's more cheering and more flashbulbs popping tonight than I've seen in a while.

Michael is still crowding the plate, then opening up with his front foot and shoulder. Why doesn't someone tell him to back off the plate and step into the ball like his own baseball hero,

ROOKIE

Roberto Clemente, who stood as far as possible from the plate and then strode aggressively toward it? Batting again in the third, Michael swings at the first pitch and loops a soft easy-out liner to right field. In the fifth he looks bad on strike two; then, bailing out, is helpless as called strike three nicks the outside corner. (The fans jeer the umpire.) Maybe he does have potential, but for now every other player on the field is more authoritative than Michael at the plate.

In the seventh he hits a bouncer to the shortstop on the first pitch, easy out at first, and with the score 8–3 and Michael not likely to bat again, a large chunk of the crowd heads for the exits.

The Cubs tie the game, sending us to extra innings again, and Michael drives in the go-ahead run in the tenth with a double past third base. Alas, Orlando comes back with two runs in the bottom of the inning to win the game and steal his headlines.

No sign of Pete Vecsey all night. Probably got his interview, flew back to New York, and is kicking back at his vacation home right now.

Michael stands at .185. Since his 17-for-52 streak at the beginning of the season brought him to .327, he's gone 47-for-291, or .161.

———

And the cynics are cattier than ever. In his notes column in the next morning's *Sentinel*, Larry Guest refers to the recent bust of Cleveland Indians slugger Albert Belle for using a corked bat, then asks, "Won't somebody puh-leeze show Michael Jordan how to cork his bat? . . . While on the subject of Error Jordan, lemme see if I can understand this. Michael can't hit, can't play defense, can't run the bases, and won't sign autographs for the fans. MJ surely must have compromising photos of somebody in the White Sox's front office."

The Struggle Continues

Cheap shots. I still don't understand these people who insist Michael shouldn't be playing, as long as he wants to do it and it's OK by the White Sox. You can't fault him for pursuing a dream, and if the White Sox didn't believe there was at least a chance of him amounting to something someday, they'd give his spot to someone who does have a chance. I'll see it differently if the Sox call him up in September instead of a more deserving prospect, but for now Michael is just a guy doing what he wants to do, with the blessing of the Sox chiefs, and what's wrong with that?

I do chuckle over one note in the *Sentinel*'s coverage, though I'm pretty sure it's not meant as a joke. The reporter quotes an unnamed member of the Barons' organization, "I've been here three months and I haven't spoken to [Michael]. But he's a great guy."

Michael Flexes His Muscle

"Sacrificers are not the ones to pity. The ones to pity are those they sacrifice."

— Elizabeth Bowen, *The Death of the Heart*

As the Barons loosen up out in left field before the last game of the series, I hang around the dugout hoping for a chance to ask Terry Francona about that interview I requested a while back. He'd been friendly, if wary, and said that if he got Michael's approval he'd give me all the time I wanted.

I'm alone in the dugout when Francona comes out of the runway from the clubhouse.

"Hi, Terry. Remember me?"

"Yeah, how ya doin'?" We shake.

"Did you get the OK for an interview?"

"Wellll," he says, working some chew into his mouth as we sit down on the bench. "I talked to Michael about it, and his story was a little different from yours. He said your book is unauthorized."

Imagine my surprise.

"Michael didn't tell me *not* to do it," Terry says. "But he would rather I didn't."

"So, does that mean you're going to stay out of it?"

"Yeah," Terry says, loosing a stream of chew-juice, "I'd rather just stay out of it. I don't need to be in any book."

Michael Flexes His Muscle

"Would you do an interview about yourself, your life in baseball, minor-league life in general?"

"Nah. I'm not trying to be a hardass about it, but I don't need to be in any *book*. I'm just a Double-A manager. Before this happened nobody knew who I was, and I'd just as soon keep it that way. We're not doing too good as a team, and I'd just as soon focus my energy on what's going on out on the field. That's kind of gotten lost in all this." He looks at me and repeats, "Nah, I don't need to be in any *book*."

I shrug. I can't really blame Francona. Nobody wants to displease a potentate.

With nothing left to say, we're sitting there uncomfortably for a couple of minutes, side by side, staring out at the non-action on the field, until a local TV reporter requesting a short interview affords Francona the chance to ditch me. Francona follows him to the other end of the dugout, where a cameraman awaits.

I start jotting down notes on our exchange, but decide to move down the bench on the off chance he'll tell the TV man something interesting.

No, it's the same riff he's given reporters all season, about how the only thing he's ever seen remotely like Michaelmania was when he was Pete Rose's teammate on the Montreal Expos, back when Rose was chasing Ty Cobb's all-time record for hits . . . People are drawn to heroes, blah blah blah . . . Zzzzzzz . . . I go back to making notes on our conversation.

Suddenly: "You're not taking this down, are you?!"

Huh? I look up, startled. Even as the TV tape rolls, Francona, who didn't want to be a hardass, is glaring at me, all shook up.

"Ummm . . . no, I'm not"—aside from the fact that I've got

ROOKIE

a legitimate press pass hanging around my neck and have a perfect right to be here.

Finally Francona turns back to the reporter and resumes the interview. "Michael shows up on time, he works hard, and he's a great guy. There's not much more you can say."

They take pains to deprive me of *this*? I sit there wondering what in the world Francona's been told about me.

The interview finished, Francona heads out to the field. The TV reporter turns to me with a smile and says, "'You're not taking this down, are you?'"

Michael, Michael, Michael. (Mister Falk, Mister Falk, Mister Falk.) You reduce a grown man to a jumpy minion without giving it a second thought—on the presumption, one can only conclude, that your life and fortunes are more important than his.

So What Are Three Rings Worth?

*"Pride, like the magnet, constantly points to one object,
self; but, unlike the magnet, it has no attractive pole,
but at all points repels."*

— Charles Caleb Colton, *Lacon*

Pete Vecsey's interview with Michael appears in the *New York Post* on Friday, July 29, four days after we watched the game in Orlando together. According to Vecsey, he snagged Michael after the game at the Barons' hotel and spent four hours with him.

Michael's arrogance is a turnoff, his bitterness simply sad.

He says he sometimes told his Bulls teammates, during the latter part of the 1992–93 season, that he had lost interest and was considering retirement. And his father was telling him to pack it in. "He felt my teammates didn't appreciate what I was doing for them." Vecsey says Michael referred specifically to Scottie Pippen and Horace Grant.

"I covered their asses when they got tight at the end of games and I had to overcome fourth-quarter deficits all by myself. It bothered my father a lot, just as it bothered me, to hear them bitchin' about not getting enough credit, or not getting enough shots, or squawking about the supposed preferential treatment I was getting from Phil [Jackson, Bulls head coach].

ROOKIE

" . . . They had no idea how much pressure and grief I had to put up with off the court. I wanted them to find out how tough it was to be on their own. Scottie found out the hard way what it's like to be under the microscope twenty-four hours a day."

He liked Phil Jackson—with reservations. "What I objected to was Phil's insistence to diversify the offense. Each year he stressed that more and more. I didn't like it, because it put more pressure on me to produce at crunch time after being out of rhythm most of the game." Three championships or no . . .

It gets worse. The same guy who scoffs at the notion that he received preferential treatment says that not long before announcing his retirement last fall, he talked to Bulls GM Jerry Krause about his "disinterest in playing the regular season," as Vecsey puts it. "If Phil could have come up with something, I might have stayed. If I could have sat for a large portion of the regular season, the way Bill Cartwright did [Cartwright was in his mid-thirties and on the injured list as often as not], I would have stayed. But Phil couldn't come up with a reason why I should stay.

"Let's face it, if I was allowed to sit out until a month before the playoffs, something like that, the media would have been all over me. They would have said, 'Who does he think he is? He thinks he's above the game. He's not a team player! He's selfish!' All those things." Unreasonable bastards . . .

He can't think of anything that could make him come back now. If he drops baseball, there's always golf to kill the boredom. "Money? I've got ten-year deals with most of my sponsors, and I'm only in the second or third year with most of them. Even if I could [think of a reason to come back], my pride would stop me. I'd never want the media to think they were right. Most of 'em predicted I'd be back. Well, I won't. I still love the actual game, but I hate many aspects surrounding it. I'll play in charity and pickup games, but I'll never play organized ball again."

———

It leaves a bad taste. And it's sad that after all Michael accomplished in basketball, all the highs for him and for us, he's left with this joylessness, this bitterness toward former teammates, all of it. And once more there's this strange fixation on the media, on proving 'em wrong.

The interview strikes others the same way it strikes me. *Time* magazine runs an item on its "People" page under the heading, "Why, Those Ingrates, I'm Too Good for 'Em!" and cites Michael's comment, "They had no idea how much pressure and grief I had to put up with off the court while carrying them on the court. I wanted them to find out for themselves how tough it was to be on their own."

Time didn't add any commentary. None needed.

Michael Goes Deep

"Few things are impossible to diligence and skill."
— Samuel Johnson, *Rasselas*

The networks don't interrupt regularly scheduled programs to break the news, but Keith Olbermann makes the long-awaited announcement as the last item on late-night *SportsCenter*, Saturday, July 30. In Hoover, Alabama this evening, in front of the latest "biggest crowd of the season" at Hoover Metropolitan Stadium (13,751), Michael Jordan, in his 354th professional at-bat, cracked his first "big fly," a 370-foot dinger off Kevin Rychel of the Carolina Mudcats.

Alas, by the time he connected in the eighth inning, the local TV cameramen had gone home. Unless a fan happened to be videotaping—unknown, as yet—the historic moment is lost.

———

In Chattanooga the night after the blast (he also had a double), Michael goes 2-for-3 in front of 9,827 fans at Historic Engel Stadium. The mini-streak lifts him to only .193, but as Terry Francona tells the press, "The whole idea in the minor leagues is to improve. At the end of the year, we look to see where a player is, compared to the beginning."

Michael speaks about his recent flurry. "I've been more sure of myself at the plate in the last week. I've just tried to make

Michael Goes Deep

sure the ball is in the strike zone or close to it, and then try to get wood on the ball."

About the dinger, "I don't look for power. I try to make contact and use my speed. Some guys have the size to be power hitters. I think I have more of a speed-and-finesse style of game."

And, adding a dash of humility, "I think my teammates have been very supportive of me all year. To see me meet the ultimate challenge of hitting a home run made them happy, and that made me feel real good."

———

By now Stu Ganz is back home in Sunnyvale, California. Ganz, forty-six, is a cable-TV ad executive and, on the side, the ring announcer for the World Wrestling Federation in the Bay Area. He's also a longtime video nut who, vacationing in Athens, Alabama the last couple of weeks, attended Saturday night's game and captured Michael's moment from his seat on the first-base side, about twenty rows up. With his wife and kids staying on in Alabama, Ganz flew back to California on Sunday; he had to be back at work on Monday.

Monday morning, 7 A.M. Pacific time, Ganz is awakened by a call from his wife. The Barons, over a Birmingham radio station, have put out an allpoints bulletin for a tape of the Jordan homer.

"So I call the Barons and talk to Frank Buccieri, the PR guy," Ganz tells me later. "The first thing out of his mouth, literally, is, 'We're really interested in the tape but we don't have any cash to offer. We'd like to get you an autographed ball, but we can't promise anything at all.' [The Barons' version is that the first words out of Ganz's mouth when he called were, "I've got the tape—what can I get for it?"] I told him I'd be glad to send

ROOKIE

it to them if I could maybe give it to Michael myself, or get an autographed ball or something. He said they'd try but they couldn't promise anything.

"I went ahead and told him OK. Must have been jet lag. I talked to a bunch of friends in the next hour—it's still only eight in the morning—and they all said, 'You're not just going to send that tape out for nothing? That doesn't sound like you! How about ESPN, *Hard Copy, Current Affair?*' So I start thinking maybe I should hold off. I start making some calls."

Ganz doesn't make it to work until he's called *ET, Current Affair*, and *Hard Copy*.

Hard Copy is interested. Ganz tells them, "Of course, I want to be part of the piece."

Hard Copy says, "Of course, we wanted to include an interview with you." A deal is struck: for a sum in "the low four figures," *Hard Copy* gets a two-week exclusive on Ganz's tape. They'll fly Ganz down to L.A. when he gets off work the next day, Tuesday, pick him up and drive him to Paramount, where they'll make a copy of his video and sit him down for a short interview.

Ganz calls Frank Buccieri back with the news. By now several people have called the club saying they had videotaped Michael's homer, but the Barons haven't seen anything yet. Frank tells Stu Ganz to please call back when the *Hard Copy* exclusive is up in two weeks.

On Tuesday the *San Jose Mercury-News*, Ganz's local paper, runs a wire-service item saying the Birmingham Barons are hoping a fan videotaped Michael Jordan's first homer. Ganz calls in saying *he* did. The paper sends a reporter over to his office for an interview.

Ganz flies down to L.A. after work, takes a *Hard Copy* limo out to Paramount, does his bit. *Hard Copy* tells Ganz they hope to do a "final chapter" to the story later, with Ganz making an in-person presentation of the videotape to Michael. Ganz takes a cab to the Universal Hilton, orders room service, watches pay-per-view movies until he falls asleep, and catches a 7 A.M. flight home.

Where he finds he's been trashed by the *Mercury-News* in a story called "Milking Michael's Homer."

But ink is ink, as they say. Ganz, suddenly receiving calls from reporters all over the U.S. and as far away as Australia, isn't complaining. He doesn't feel guilty anyway, and even Barons president Bill Hardekopf, on a radio talk-show hookup with Ganz, concedes there's nothing wrong with Ganz selling his videotape—he bought a ticket, he shot his own video, he can do what he wants. "We just didn't want to get into a bidding war," Hardekopf says. "We weren't intending to market the tape in any way. We just wanted to be able to give it to Michael and say, 'Here's your first home run.'"

It's Stu Ganz's fifteen minutes of fame. On Thursday evening, August 4, the local ABC affiliate sends a crew to his house to film the *auteur* and some chums watching the world premiere of Michael's home run on *Hard Copy*. The piece will run on the 11 P.M. news.

At last, five days after the fact, *Hard Copy* shows the world "the Ganz tape": a little jiggly, but there's Michael lashing at the pitch, the ball flying off into the night; there he is rounding third and heading home, pointing at his wife, mother, brother, and sister in the stands—and then skyward, just as we'd read in the papers, in tribute to his father, who would have turned fifty-eight the next day.

We see that Michael was *not* mobbed at the plate by the entire team, as the papers glammed it up, but simply high-fived two teammates and the batboy and continued on to the dugout as if he hit home runs every day.

But you can imagine how he was feeling, and even *this* hard-nosed scribe feels happy for him.

Ganz and his friends make the late newscast. Bob Fitzgerald of the *Hayward Argus* promptly writes a piece calling Ganz "slimy" for selling his tape to *Hard Copy* instead of giving it to Michael, saying Ganz is as bad as the greedy major-league players we abhor. Ganz phones Fitzgerald's radio program and starts a three-hour debate among listeners. "Lots of people agreed with me," he tells me later.

He's definitely got a supporter in syndicated columnist Mitch Albom, who applauds Ganz on ESPN's *The Sports Reporters* for "turning the tables" on the big-time athlete who wants something from Joe Fan for a change.

ESPN has made arrangements, in the event of a major-league strike, to fill its Sunday-night baseball slots with Barons games on August 14 and 21. A few days before the first game, Stu Ganz hears that the network plans to run a pregame interview with Michael. What a perfect time to show the homer tape! Ganz gets a release from *Hard Copy*, which owns exclusive rights for a few more days, and calls ESPN.

"They wanted the tape," Ganz says later, "but they were talking, like, $500. They didn't want to pay the price."

What was the price?

"I told 'em ten thousand. I hoped to get two or three. But with them talking only a few hundred, I didn't think it was worth it."

———

Ganz calls Nike, thinking the shoemakers could use the tape in a commercial, but nothing comes of it. Upper Deck cards expresses some interest in buying a few still pictures from the tape, but nothing comes of it. Gatorade isn't interested. *Hard*

Michael Goes Deep

Copy never arranges for Ganz to personally present Michael with a copy of his videotape.

Ganz is left with that low-four-figures score from *Hard Copy* and a scrapbook full of clippings. "I left a message on Frank Buccieri's voicemail after *Hard Copy*'s two-week exclusive ran out," he says later, "but I never heard back from the Barons. I was going to give Michael a copy then, free. I was never trying to hold him up."

In the week after Michael's clout, several fans send in *their* video versions, which the Barons collect on one tape and present to Michael. The fans get autographed balls, after all.

Ganz never does send the Barons his tape. He keeps expecting them to call him. He's positive he's got the best version of the historic moment. And positive, apparently, that it *was* an historic moment.

A Few Days in
Patton Valley

*"It is better to be hated for what you are than loved for
what you are not."*

— André Gide

Michael's batting .190 when the Barons come to Greenville,
South Carolina on August 4, but there's an overflow crowd of
7,167 at Greenville Municipal Stadium. The Braves' PR man
didn't get 150 requests for credentials like the first time
around, but the sixty he did get will make for a much livelier
press box than the usual outfit: the beat writer, a radio jock or
two, and a couple of TV guys (for a few innings).

The stadium, though located in a desolate spot at the edge of
town, is a quaint, beautiful one. Perfectly symmetrical: the
same distance down the left- and right-field lines; bleachers
running from halfway down the left-field line to halfway down
the right-field line; the glassed-in press box directly behind the
plate. Even the signs around the outfield fences are perfect:
two rows high from foul pole to foul pole, the only irregularity
being a space in right center, about the width of two signs,
where the big scoreboard rises up.

The G-Braves are orderly and symmetrical even during the
national anthem: the right fielder standing with the first baseman at first, the left fielder with the third baseman at third, and

A Few Days in Patton Valley

the center fielder flanked by the shortstop and second baseman at second; the pitcher on the mound; the catcher directly behind the plate, flanked by the two umpires, who can't help but fall into formation.

Michael still looks overmatched in the batter's box. And frustrated. He pops out his first time up. The second time he looks miffed on a called strike, and after popping out again on the next pitch, grouses at the umpire on his way back to the dugout.

Defensively, he's now a left fielder. He's got potential as a ballhawk—covers ground, and has cut down on his errors—but the coaching staff has conceded he doesn't have the throwing arm a right fielder needs.

In the seventh inning Michael manages a base hit when his grounder pulls the first baseman well off the bag and the pitcher, taking the throw, stumbles and can't make the play.

But it will look like any other single in the box score, and after Michael whacks a sharp single in the ninth, the 2-for-4 has him back up to .193.

———

Friday night, Bat Night, is like every other night in the minor leagues, numbingly familiar yet oddly idyllic: one team playing catch on the outfield grass while the other takes batting practice; idle joshing and chatter around the batting cage; some ex–major leaguer, in this case Greenville's weathered but exuberant Bruce Dal Canton (a 51–49 pitcher in eleven seasons) throwing BP from behind a screen. At 5:30 sharp the G-Braves gather up their batting-practice balls, dump them in the big canvas bag and clear the field for the Barons.

Terry Francona carries the Barons' ballbag out behind the screen and, waving leadoff man Doug Brady into the cage,

ROOKIE

throws the first of two or three hundred pitches, three rounds for each guy all the way down the order. Mike Barnett, down on one knee behind the cage, peers through the mesh studying every stroke as if it's rocket science, stirring only to eject some chew-juice or to offer a little advice to a Baron exiting the cage. Country music sounds over the PA—Clint Black, then a twangy version of "Piece of My Heart." A half-dozen faintly whiskered G-Braves sign autographs along the railings, guys with a good shot at being junior-high gym teachers in a couple of years—if they're lucky.

Michael, focussed, takes his batting-practice hacks without saying much to anyone. Mike Barnett, watching him intently, rises from his knee between rounds and comes over with some encouragement: *That's good; rap 'em out . . .*

As Michael walks back to the dugout to pick up his mitt after his last cuts, the kids in the first row are yelling at him, begging for his autograph on balls and gloves and programs. "Michael, *pleeeze!*" Today he at least looks up, gives them a little smile and says, "I can't do that now."

He spends a couple of minutes in the dugout cooling off, swigging from a paper Gatorade cup, while the kids bang on the roof with their bats and shout at him. "Michael, we know you're in there!" "If I drop my glove, will you throw it back to me?" They can't see Michael and he can't see them, though they're separated only by the dugout roof. It's a funny sight from my vantage on the field: the gleeful, screaming kids up above and Michael down below, feigning not to hear.

It's all more entertaining than the game turns out to be. After this amusing prelude, I spend three hours in the press box watching Michael go 0-for-4 with three strikeouts. He doesn't look much closer to the big leagues than he did back in May.

A Few Days in Patton Valley

It's a blissful drive from Greenville over to Mom's cottage in Franklin, North Carolina—all rocks and streams and sunlight shafting down through the trees and two bright yellow lines in the middle of the narrow winding road through the mountains. As so often happens, I'm thinking Michael ought to do something like this with his wife and kids. Leave the cellular phone home, mellow out, get into a frame of mind where you don't mind being stuck behind that Winnebago for fifteen miles, stop at some of the scenic points, check out the occasional isolated restaurants or craft shops (which Michael might actually be able to do out here, there are so few people around).

Of course he couldn't take the time, not with all the commitments a potentate has, but he's missing so much. Sure, he'll have time someday—like after these ten-year endorsement deals are over—but his kids are kids *now*.

It rains and thunderstorms for three days in Patton Valley, but just as well. The cottage is tucked so cozily between the heavy-hanging horse-chestnut trees in front and the woods on two sides that you feel like you're in a rain forest. At cocktail time you sit in one of the rockers on the front porch and actually savor the fierce yet soothing thunderstorms that clatter on the roof and bring sweet smells out of the flora and fauna. You see how many growing things you can identify within thirty feet: chestnuts, hemlocks, jack pines, white pines, white oaks, buckeyes, cedars, forsythia, lilac.

On the nature path that cuts through the woods up to Aunt Helen's place, when the storm finally breaks, water drips from the leaves of ironwood and tulip poplar and dogwood trees. The undergrowth is a tangle of wild-grape vines, pokeweed, butterfly weed, Joe-Pye weed, Queen Anne's lace, black-eyed Susan, black snakeroot, trillium, lady's slippers, and four kinds of pussytoes, not to mention the despised but heavenly-smelling honeysuckle. As every year, Aunt Helen's yard and garden are resplendent with most of these species plus her beloved "fragrants"—sourwood trees and olive bushes—and daisies and tall, elegant, white beetleweed.

It's not Chicago or L.A., not even Greenville or Chattanooga. But so much the better, sometimes. Waking up in the middle of the night and walking out to take a squirt off the front porch, you find it pitch-black outside, nothing but a couple of lonely country-road streetlights in the distance; no sound but the monotonous, deafening whine of a million katydids and the water running into the pond down the hill and the occasional *burrrp* of a bullfrog. In the huge night, out in the middle of nowhere, you can't help but be reminded of your tiny place in the scheme of things.

Come on up, Michael. Sit on the porch for a few days—no phones, no Mister Falk—and listen to the sounds and contemplate your place. It'll be good . . .

———

Over in Wedowee, Alabama, where high-school principal Hulond Humphries vetoed interracial dates at the prom a few months ago, the school burns to the ground hours before demonstrations by the Southern Christian Leadership Conference and the Ku Klux Klan. As the fire rages, the infamous Humphries and other whites pummel a black TV cameraman, who in turn sues Humphries and the school board.

Humphries has been reassigned, and Federal marshals are now conspicuous in Wedowee, a speck of 800 souls between Atlanta and Birmingham.

———

The big sports story, if you want to call it that, is the imminent major-league players' strike.

A Few Days in Patton Valley

It's only a story if you care, and who cares anymore? Who can sympathize? Baseball brings in millions or billions of dollars every year. There's plenty for owners and players alike, and the public doesn't much care how they split it up. The public wants ballgames in the summertime, statistics, pennant races, record chases, stories about stars. The public counts on baseball for escape, not for more of what we get in real life: malevolent-looking men in ties posturing in the media over power and money.

It's one of the most exciting major-league seasons in a long time, and as always there's plenty worth escaping in the real-life news, but we're fed up with baseball's in-house problems—the ego, the hubris, the greed—and we don't really care if they strike or not. Life will go on. We just wish they'd quit talking about it.

I don't know about the kids who supposedly worship these guys, but they'll survive too, and probably be better off for learning early that sports heroes have the same unbecoming appetites as anyone else.

———

Michael Jordan, who dares not ruffle any feathers, has a pat response to questions about a possible work stoppage. "That's the major leagues. This is the minor leagues."

Looking for Meaning in Memphis

"Kings are like stars—they rise and set, they have
The worship of the world, but no repose."

— Shelley, *Hellas*

Anticipating the big-league strike on August 12, ESPN made arrangements to fill two Sunday-night baseball slots with Barons games, August 14 and 21. The first one is in Memphis, and I make the seven-hour drive over as soon as the strike's a sure thing—two days early—even though I could hang in Signal Mountain and watch on TV. It's *Memphis*. Besides, Michael smacked another homer a few days ago—he's getting more intriguing.

It's the height of Elvis Week, seventeen years since he reportedly expired. All kinds of events going on, from a five-kilometer road-race to bus tours down to The King's boyhood home in Tupelo, Mississippi, leading up to the candlelight vigil at Graceland on Monday night, the actual anniversary of his untimely (rumored) demise.

I decide to make the Graceland tour. Many expect Elvis to materialize this week, and maybe I'll get the exclusive. I've got a better chance of talking to him than to our latest wayward icon.

It's overcast and muggy as I find my way to Elvis Presley

Boulevard, otherwise known as Highway 51. The stretch near Graceland was probably nice and peaceful when Elvis moved in in 1957, but now it's a row of car lots and fast-food joints and such establishments as "Elvis Presley Boulevard Pawn" and a liquor store with a sign swearing, "Elvis shopped here, really!"

Then suddenly you see these two *jets* right there by the road—the *Lisa Marie* and *Hound Dog II*—and signs directing you into the vast Graceland parking lot.

After buying my ticket and checking out Rockabilly's diner, the Heartbreak Hotel restaurant, the Good Rockin' record store, the Welcome to My World gift shop, the Elvis Threads apparel shop, the Walk a Mile in My Shoes theater, the Sincerely Elvis Museum, and the Elvis Presley Automobile Museum, I board a shuttle bus that carries a couple dozen of us across the boulevard and up a long driveway to the house.

It's a precision operation. While my group listens to our tour guide's first spiel in the front hallway, the bored-looking security guard, one of the 400 Graceland employees, tells me everything is timed to the minute. Sure enough, there's another group coming in behind us as our youthful guide finishes her first bit and leads us on.

As I've always heard, Graceland is a monument to conspicuous consumption and bad taste. The bedroom suite upstairs, where The King so ignominiously met his maker, is closed to the public, but we see the game room with three color TVs side-by-side (so Elvis could watch three football games at once); the countless wet bars; the god-awful Jungle Room, done in hideous rugs and bizarre furniture and trophy horns of various beasts, where our sweet young guide coos, "Elvis decorated this his-self"; a room where El, under the influence of who-knows-what, had the ceiling carpeted ("It made the room acoustically sound, and Elvis recorded two albums here").

ROOKIE

We're taken down a narrow stairway whose walls *and* sloping ceiling are lined with mirrors; you've got to hold on to the rail, you're so dizzy from the assault of images.

Oh, you King.

But long live The King. By the time the tour ends and I take the shuttle bus back and walk out to my car, the vast parking lot is nearly full.

Nearly a million people a year still pay to visit this dead man's former dwelling, so long after he dropped out of sight. We're talking *fame* here.

And I can't help thinking about what that kind of fame, with all the riches and yes-men and bigger-than-lifeness, did to Elvis. Somewhere in there, he lost his way.

Reminds me of someone I met once.

———

Two huge ESPN trucks sit in front of Tim McCarver Stadium when I show up on Sunday afternoon, and though it's two hours before gametime, there's a fair crowd inside.

The only problem, I find, is that Michael isn't playing tonight. He hurt his shoulder diving for a fly ball on Friday night and will undergo an MRI in Birmingham on Monday morning. He'll miss five games, minimum.

If I were paranoid, I'd think they were toying with me after I drove seven hours to Memphis.

I chat with Chicks president Dave Hersh, who's turned out in a double-breasted navy-blue blazer and is wielding one of his batonlike cigars. A promotor (of his team and himself) to the marrow, he's enjoying this: his Chicks on ESPN tonight, himself on the *Today* show tomorrow morning to talk about the major-league strike and the minor leagues in general.

I move on to Chicks manager Ron Johnson, who's talking to

Looking for Meaning in Memphis

a reporter about tonight's nationally televised game. "Oh, yeah, these kids are excited as heck, even though we had a long bus ride last night after the game was rescheduled for ESPN. They want their families and friends to see 'em. They wanna do well. You won't see 'tired' tonight. But stick around tomorrow—that'll probably be one of the worst games in the history of baseball."

Johnson laments the major-league strike. "You know what I hate the most? Guys who've had a good year here are looking forward to call-ups when the big leagues expand their rosters in September, and right now that's not going to happen. I feel sorry for them because I was a very borderline player, and when I got called up in September of 1982 it was the most exciting thing of my life. A highlight of my career? If you know my career, you know that was *the* highlight. My dad drove to Kansas City and walked into the clubhouse, the whole thing. You never know what's going to happen from year to year—a kid might have a great year this year, but then he gets hurt next year and he may never get the opportunity again."

A kid named Strickland trots by. Johnson says, "Here's one of my younger guys. Hey, Strick, you excited about tonight's game?"

The kid deadpans as he passes, "Nah, just another game," and we all laugh.

"Look at 'em," Johnson says. "Haircuts, shaved real nice, lookin' good . . . " Then his smile disappears and he's back to the reason for the nerves and the haircuts. "I'm sure both the major-league players and the owners have good reasons for what they're doing, but I'm like you: I'm down here. I know what twenty bucks is, but I can't fathom what a million is."

———

ROOKIE

As polka music plays over the PA system and the Chickasaw Indian mascot highsteps ridiculously on top of one dugout and then the other, the ESPN crew hangs out near the first-base dugout, waiting to do their pregame spots. The ebullient Joe Morgan, the greatest second baseman ever and nowadays a very good TV analyst, bounces around joking with one person after another, loose as can be, frequently bursting into his infectious laugh. The skinny end of his tie hangs lower than the fat end, but you can tell he doesn't sweat such things; when he buttons his blazer for the camera it won't show anyway.

Curt Bloom, the radio man, has his eye on ESPN's Jon Miller, one of baseball's premier play-by-play announcers. "The best in the business," says C.B., who aspires to climb the ladder. "But I'm in competition with myself, to be the best announcer *I* can be. There are a lot of great ones, and if I worried about 'em all, I would have gotten out a long time ago. I'm competing with myself."

Has Michael's presence had any impact on his career?

"*Oh* yeah. The two home-run calls, people hearing the 'Gone-zo!'—yeah. Michael brought me the opportunity to be heard in Chicago and wherever else they played the home-run tape. But," he adds modestly, "I don't want people to get the misconception . . . I mean, they weren't hearing *me*, they were hearing Michael Jordan's home run. He hit the home run; I didn't do anything."

"But you made the call. Hitting homers is his thing; calling 'em is yours. That call is your moment, too."

"Welll . . ." C.B. chuckles, thinking back; it's a fond memory. "I'll never forget the first dinger. The story behind it is that in his previous two at-bats Michael had come so close, and when it happened I was so excited . . .

Looking for Meaning in Memphis

"They all make fun of me, they all goof on me about it, but my home-run call is 'Gone-zo! Gone-zo, Tremie! Gone-zo, DeSarcina!' Whoever. So that was it. I remember saying, 'Long fly ball, deep to left field, Ratliff going back . . . at the warning track . . . it's *gone*-zo, Jordan!'"

That's one tape C.B.'s sure to send out with his resumé this winter.

———

Besides ESPN's broadcast crew, there's a small crew from ESPN2 here doing a feature, and people from the *New York Times*, the *Washington Post*, the *Chicago Sun-Times*, and the *Kansas City Star*. There's a certain big-league atmosphere, but once the game starts—without Michael—it feels different from any game I've seen this summer, precisely because it's truly minor-league: a bunch of unknowns playing hard, hoping to make the least little name for themselves. It's nice. Somehow, because Michael isn't overshadowing everything else, you get more involved in the game, you look more closely at all the other guys on both sides.

It's a great game. The Barons take an early 2–0 lead on a homer by Troy Fryman, and left-hander Mike Bertotti has a two-hit shutout going into the eighth. Then some classic minor-league ball livens things up. After a Chicks double, the Barons' shortstop scoops up a slow roller and throws it over the first baseman's head. The left fielder misjudges a fly ball; it rolls to the fence, both runners score, game tied. The Chicks score once more to take a 3–2 lead into the ninth, the Barons' last chance.

The Barons come back with three to take a 5–3 lead.

But in the bottom of the ninth the Chicks score once to close to 5–4 and load the bases with two outs—only to expire, not

ROOKIE

without one last thrill, as a long, high blast finally drops into the glove of center fielder Kerry Valrie up against the fence.

———

Heading ninety miles south of Memphis to Oxford, Mississippi on Monday morning, I muse on the irony of Michael's basketball-playing making him wildly rich and famous and a hero even in his own mind. Oxford's William Faulkner, one of *my* heroes, lived in debt and was known to his neighbors as "Count No-'Count" even as he turned out works of genius on his way to the Nobel Prize.

Reaching Oxford, the home of the University of Mississippi but still a small town, I try to forget the Shoney's and McDonald's and Subway that stand on the main drag today, and imagine all this as Faulkner country, home of Lucas Beauchamp and Reverend Hightower and the Snopeses and all the rest. And I *can*, back in the quiet, shady neighborhoods, with phrases like "the hot still pinewiney silence of the August afternoon" filling my head.

I find Faulkner's old place, Rowan Oak, at a secluded, wooded bend in Old Taylor Road. I park down a narrow dirt road into the woods, where there's room for a few cars, and walk back up the road and through a big iron gate and then follow a long, long S-shaped aisle of stately cedar trees up to the house. William Faulkner's place! He bought it in 1930, run-down, for $6,000, and still owned it when he died in 1962: a big white two-story with green trim and grand, Old South columns in front. I'm greeted at the door by a young Ole Miss graduate student who tells me Rowan Oak is now owned and operated by the university. Needless to say, it's nothing like the attraction Graceland is.

It couldn't be more different from Graceland. Spacious

Looking for Meaning in Memphis

enough, surely, but spare: everything functional, nothing un-necessary. Downstairs there's the library where Faulkner sometimes worked, with one of his pipes lying on the desk. In back is the room where he wrote the Pulitzer-winning *A Fable* (the outline written on the wall in Faulkner's tiny scrawl), with a frayed rug on the floor and a single bare light bulb on the ceiling and Faulkner's reading glasses on the table next to his old Underwood typewriter. Upstairs, sparely furnished bed-rooms (a pair of Faulkner's worn khaki work pants folded on his bed) open off a hallway that runs the length of the house and leads out to a little terrace in front.

Outside, Rowan Oak comprises several acres of pastures and fields, a stable, and various other little outbuildings, including one I recognize from a poignant photo of Faulkner, white-haired and frail, near the end of his life. Walking around the atmospheric grounds—where, I'm told, the college boys like to bring girls on warm spring nights—I imagine the great man wandering around out here under the stars, whiskied up, smelling the country smells and hearing, even over the din of katydids, the voices he heard.

Walking back to my car (in "the hot still pinewiney silence of the August afternoon," indeed), I recall what Rowan Oak's curator said in a piece on writers' homes in *Southern Living*. "There's nothing pretentious about this place. Mr. William lived rather plainly. He didn't have much interest in *things*."

———

As advertised, general-admission tickets for Monday night's game sell for Michael's current batting average, .192—$1.92—even though he's not here.

Leaving the park afterward, I think about cruising by the candlelight vigil at Graceland—but think better of it. Good thing. More than 12,000 people turn out between 9 P.M. and dawn, bearing flowers and wreaths and other offerings. In the dark, with the King's romantic hits playing over outdoor speakers, they climb the long, winding driveway and go around back to leave their bouquets and remembrances on the gravesite in the Meditation Gardens, where Elvis (if he's really in there) lies with his parents.

———

Tuesday I spend two and a half hours at the Lorraine Motel, where Martin Luther King took the fatal bullet. It's now the impressive and controversial National Civil Rights Museum. You first walk through a big room with a special exhibition on the old Negro Leagues, then move through everything from the early Ku Klux Klan to burnt-out buses from the Freedom Rides.

The end of the tour takes you down a short second-floor hall for an eerie look (through glass) into the rooms King and his entourage occupied on that fateful day in April 1968, their habituation "re-created" with dirty coffee cups and ashtrays full of butts and unmade beds and a copy of the April 4, 1968 *Memphis Press-Scimitar*. In the parking lot below, the two big white cars they arrived in remain exactly where they were parked.

I remember being a high-school freshman in northern Virginia, sitting in my bedroom listening to the report that Frank "Hondo" Howard of our Washington Senators (now the Texas Rangers) had just tied a major-league record by blasting his tenth home run in six games—only to have that bulletin superseded by the one from Memphis.

Heading back to my car, I pick up a pamphlet from Jacqueline Smith, the black woman who sits on a worn-out couch

Looking for Meaning in Memphis

on the sidewalk across the street every day of the year protesting the museum. "They're trampling on Dr. King's legacy with this Disneyland approach," she says. Her pamphlet calls the museum "a disgrace to the life and works of Dr. King, a scam and a landgrab."

Scanning the pamphlet back in my car, I spot an excerpt from M.L.K.'s final sermon about how he hoped to be remembered: "Say that I was a drum major for justice. Say that I was a drum major for peace. I was a drum major for righteousness.

"And all the other shallow things will not matter. I won't have any money to leave behind. I won't have the fine and luxurious things of life to leave behind. But I just want to leave a committed life behind."

———

Item from The *New York Times* News Syndicate: "The sports film company, Sports Legends Inc., has filed a $1 million lawsuit against Michael Jordan and his agent, contending the former basketball star is blocking reuse of a 1987 interview with Simpson.

"Jordan, who appears for 63 seconds of the original 32-minute film, must be compensated if his name is used in the proposed Simpson video, Jordan's agent, David Falk, is quoted as saying."

Eureka!

"The secret of success is constancy to purpose."
— Benjamin Disraeli

Last week in August, last home stand of the season at Hoover Metroplitan Stadium. Now that the end is nigh, it all seems to have passed in a flash, despite my tribulations with Michael and Mister Falk and the Barons. The kids go back to school next week—it seems they busted out for the summer only last week. And it's full-time football time down South now. This week, in the Volunteer spirit, Tennesseans 10,000 strong are making a cross-country bus caravan to attend the Big Orange opener at UCLA; down here, Auburn and 'Bama will bring the entire state to a halt on Saturday. In the evenings now the light has the first traces of that dreamy autumnal glow, and sometimes the humidity breaks enough for you to imagine cool fall days, yellow leaves, winter beyond.

It will be a week of ceremonies and festivities at Hoover Stadium. This evening, Frank Buccieri sets up a microphone in the grass behind home plate, and team president Bill Hardekopf introduces a dozen or so Middle Americans lined up behind him. They turn out to be the mayors of Birmingham and Hoover and the surrounding towns of Irondale, Jasper, Leeds (Charles Barkley's hometown), Vestavia Hills, and Warrior, plus two men from the Shelby County Economic Council.

Eureka!

For the record, it's a ceremony to honor Michael Jordan for the impact his presence has had on the local economy this summer. It's really a photo-op for the mayors, a chance for them to meet Michael, and a chance for the Barons to dress up the last few days of what they're calling "this very special season in Birmingham," maybe get a mention on TV.

Michael doesn't even come out of the dugout until each mayor has been introduced and come forth and handed Hardekopf, for Michael, the mythical key to his or her fair community. When he does appear, to thunderous applause, he never approaches the mike but walks down the line shaking each hand and doling out a schmoozy smile and a few words to each small-town bigwig. A minute later, after standing in the middle of the group and saying cheese for a picture, he's on his way back to the dugout, ready to play ball.

It's a bore, one of ten million times he's shaken strangers' hands and offered a blank smile for a picture he'll never see. Of course, every one of those mayors has already ordered a copy, and even if they personally don't look good they'll frame it (not before calling the Barons to try to arrange an autograph) and hang it in their offices and tell everyone who comes in about the night they met Michael. They'll be using it in their speeches twenty years from now.

———

I can't believe what I'm seeing.

Sure, Michael cranked out his third homer the other night, in his second game back from the strained shoulder, but his average is still only .194. As he walks to the plate the first time tonight, nothing seems to have changed. The music director up in the press box cues Alan Parsons's throbbing "Sirius"—now the M.J. theme song here, even though it's as inappropriate as a

ROOKIE

leisurely "Take Me Out to the Ball Game" would be at an NBA playoff game. Michael still stands deep in the box and as close to the plate as possible—still worried about the outside pitch, apparently, despite his long arms. He's changed his stance a little, but that's nothing new; when you've got to look up to see the Mendoza Line, you try things. Tonight he looks odd up there, exaggeratedly casual: his hands are low and close to his body, his elbows sort of sagging close to his sides as if his arms are too exhausted to hold the bat up where it should be. Looks like it would take him a long time to get cranked up. As Mike Barnett would say, you don't start your swing from there.

I'm barely paying attention when Michael lashes out of that droopy-looking stance and sends a bullet to the shortstop's left. Not *far* to his left, but it's all he can do to knock it down. Michael *stung* that one.

My mind's eye re-creates the way he stood there, hunched over just slightly, hands close to his body, and smoothly back-shifted his weight as the pitcher released the ball and then brought it forward just right and snapped the bat through the hitting zone with some authority. The elusive "bat speed."

On base he's aggressive as always—stretching his lead, drawing throws from the pitcher, cramming as much experience as possible into this season. He's gotten picked off and caught stealing numerous times in the learning process, but that's what the minors are for.

After Troy Fryman advances him to second, Michael stretches his lead, leans too far toward third and nearly gets picked off again. The learning continues. *But*, you're saying to yourself after the Barons are retired and he's loping out to left-field, his long, graceful strides swallowing up ground. *Maybe. A long shot, but maybe.*

I'm watching closely when he comes up again. And for the

Eureka!

first time all season, to my eye, Michael looks truly comfortable at the plate, odd stance and all. His weight shifts smoothly back, then forward as he strides into the pitch, whips his bat through, and nails a one-hopper back to the pitcher—an easy out, but a good swing and sharp contact.

When he poles a long out to center field his third time up, I know the balls he smacked the first two times weren't accidents. He's not Roberto Clemente yet, but he's a long way from the Michael of the early season, or even last month.

———

In the sixth inning, I feel a tap on my shoulder and turn to find myself looking at Barons president Bill Hardekopf—not unexpected, since, in a spasm of beatitude over the publication of my Italy book recently, I sent an autographed copy to Chris Pika. I'm sure it got around the office.

Suddenly I rate a visit from the Barons' president. Hardekopf, a little guy who manages to look waxen despite having the permanent color of a southern Californian, speculated back in April that I might not be a writer at all. Three weeks ago he ignored the interview request I left on his voicemail. Now he asks, very politely, if I've got a few minutes to talk.

Sure I do. It's too late to make friends, but I've got time to talk.

I almost feel sorry for Bill, who's trying to convince me that all the trouble, all summer long, has been sort of a misunderstanding. If we could only rewind the film, he says, things would probably be different. Meanwhile, anything I need? An interview? Bill promises to tell me everything he told *People* and the *New York Times*.

Sure, why not? He's not Michael, but I'm not going to get

ROOKIE

Michael. Bill can fill in some blanks about the minor leagues
for me. We'll talk in his office tomorrow afternoon.

———

Suntory International hired him as president of the team on
the basis of his business and sales background. Bill, forty,
attended the University of Southern California, then spent
ten years in "consumer package-goods marketing" for Carnation and Van de Camp: "Basically you're trying to get super-
markets to stock this Van de Camp's frozen enchilada dinner,
or this Carnation breakfast bar." He next spent seven years as
an assistant athletic director in charge of marketing and promotions at USC. Suntory hired him three years ago.

Bill enthuses about his job. "For all of us here, it's two
different jobs, totally different in the off-season from what you
see now. In the off-season, October to April—and a better
term for that would be 'selling season'—that's when we dress
up and go out to all the accounts and try to sell everything
we've got to sell. Program ads. Fence signs. Concourse signs.
Grandstand signs. The radio package. Season tickets, group
tickets, the patio picnic parties, the company nights. The special events like Hat Night, Helmet Night—we have to find a
sponsor for those things. One of the most important require-
ments for being in a minor-league organization is being able to
sell. If you can't sell you won't cut it, because for half the year
you're selling."

In those months they're all essentially peers, whatever their
summertime designations—Bill, vice president Tony Ensor,
Curt Bloom, Frank Buccieri, Chris Pika, and a few others—all
salesmen putting on the smile and making calls.

Even in the summer, the distinctions don't always amount to
much. "During the five months of the season," Bill says in his

measured way (as if even this might be a dangerous subject with an "unauthorized" writer), "it's a matter of executing all the planning you've done for seven months. You're in the fire for five months. We come to work in jeans and shorts and T-shirts and we problem-solve. But it's fun. Everyone here enjoys wearing different hats and everyone pitches in. I've rolled out the tarp when it rains; I park cars and help put on promotions like everyone else.

"Minor-league baseball," Bill enthuses tepidly, "is such a *fun* industry. You can try anything. Anything goes. I think it's great."

And unlike minor-league players and managers and coaches and broadcasters and flacks who want to reach the top level, a small-businessman type like Bill is in a good enough spot right here, doing what he's probably meant to do.

He's sure not looking to risk it. I've never talked to anyone so cautious. Over and over he's told me there's been no *conspiracy* against me, nobody's been told not to talk to me about Michael, but he won't say anything I haven't heard ten times in the papers.

But there's no point in harassing Bill. He's just fronting the Barons franchise for Suntory, and taking orders from the White Sox, too. Besides, he barely knows Michael. According to Bill, there's not much more to it than walking by his locker every so often saying, "Everything OK? Let us know if you need anything."

Funny, it's exactly what Bill says to me as I'm leaving a few minutes later. "Anything else I can do? Let me know if you need anything."

"I'd like a couple of long interviews with Michael this week."

Bill smiles his wan smile. I go.

———

ROOKIE

A few hours later, before 5,324 fans, Michael keeps doing a fair impersonation of a ballplayer. First time up he legs out a grounder behind second base, covering the ninety feet in a few humongous strides. He steals second, going in with a dirt-eating Pete Rose belly flop. He barrels around to score on a sharp single, running right through the frantic stop sign of Mike Barnett, who's temporarily replacing Terry Francona in the third-base coaching box.

Second time up, Michael attacks a low pitch with a short, quick stroke and rockets a liner over the shortstop's head for an RBI single. He promptly steals second again, covering what seems like the last thirty feet with another belly slide. He looks as if he's truly feeling like a ballplayer now—not just getting dirty but accomplishing things, contributing.

In left field, he ends the fifth inning with a major-league catch, going all the way to the line and lunging at the last to make a backhand stab—looking good! When he comes out to the on-deck circle in the bottom of the inning, an older man nearby calls, "Michael, you look like a million bucks tonight!" Just as Michael turns the other way—the guy who usually pretends not to hear the fans—I see the briefest of smiles, an understandable smile of satisfaction that's erased as quickly as it appears.

At the plate he works the count, no longer going after the first reachable pitch, confident enough to take a strike, *two* strikes, looking for the one he wants. It comes, and Michael—shifting his weight back, flexing his knees slightly, shifting his weight smoothly forward, and snapping his black bat through—blasts a long double into the alley in left center. Garth Iorg would call it a *bomb*.

His first three-hit game of the season lifts him only to the Mendoza Line, but the numbers are incongruous with how good he looks right now.

Eureka!

"It's like the fourth quarter for me," Michael tells reporters afterward. "That's when you try to play your best. I'm playing my best of the season right now."

———

White Sox general manager Ron Schueler announces that Michael will play in the Florida Instructional League in September, three weeks of additional work for prospects. After that, a decision will be made about the new Arizona Fall League, where each major-league organization will send six of its top minor-leaguers for fifty competitive games. Michael is by no means a top Sox prospect, but being Michael always has its perks. They're saying the Sox will ask for some kind of special dispensation for him, and who's going to say no?

———

"If Jordan plays in '95, it should be as a Baron," declares the headline of Rubin Grant's column in the *Post-Herald*. Grant points out that while Michael is much improved at the plate, he's still far from consistent. He still commits baserunning blunders rarely seen beyond rookie leagues. Even if he plays in the instructional league and the fall league, he needs to at least open next season in Birmingham, then move up if he deserves to.

Grant concludes by saying that if Michael does return to Birmingham, "it would be nice for him to make a few public appearances, something he has seldom done this year . . . And he could show himself in the black community [Rubin Grant is black], since he is a role model for many disadvantaged black kids, and other black role models are in short supply.

"If he has time to go to some of the city's night spots, that's the least he could do."

———

ROOKIE

On the last Friday night of "this very special season" (as the PA man keeps enthusing) there's a pregame ceremony for Birmingham native Jimmy Bragan, the outgoing league president, the guy who left the drawly message on his answering machine back in April. Bragan calls his wife down, and Bill Hardekopf gives a glowing speech from a microphone behind home plate and presents an honorary Barons jersey with "BRAGAN 1" on the back. Finally, they drive out a big green John Deere tractor, a gift for Bragan's retirement to his farm. Bragan goes to the mike and effuses about the Southern League, the city of Birmingham, and "this special summer" for the Barons and the city, before handing off to Terry Francona. Francona comes out and says a few more words about the city and the fans and "this special summer" before calling Michael out, to a great roar—who jogs out, shakes Jimmy Bragan's hand, waves to the crowd, and walks back to the dugout.

Watching the late-summer light change as the first few innings pass, and thinking back over the season, I wonder where the other Barons will be next spring. What have they done for their careers in these last five months? At first they were just the anonymous background for Michael, but gradually they distinguished themselves. Chris Tremie, the stocky catcher, doesn't hit much, but catchers don't always have to hit a lot. He's got a good arm, he's a hustler—will he move up to the Triple-A Nashville Sounds next season?

First baseman Troy Fryman, who seemed at first to sag under the weight of being the younger brother of big-league star Travis Fryman, was Southern League Player of the Week a month ago and has been hitting ever since. Maybe he'll bloom.

Shortstop Glenn DiSarcina, younger brother of Angels infielder Gary, makes some fine plays and has a strong arm, but commits so many errors that his total always looks like a misprint in the statistics—where does he go from here? Recently arrived third baseman Shane Turner, thirty-one, who's had major-league trials with three teams and is playing for his fourth minor-league club *this summer*, might be on his way out of baseball; released from the Giants' organization in July, Turner happened to be available for the Barons two weeks ago when third baseman Chris Snopek broke a finger.

Outfielder-first baseman-DH Mike Robertson tore up the Southern League early, struggled in Nashville, and now is struggling here. But he's still young, he's got a good swing, and they've got hopes for him; he'll be playing ball next year.

What will any of them be doing all winter? They only get their $1,000 a month from the Sox during the season.

———

Michael, first time at bat, goes to a full count without swinging at a single pitch. I haven't seen that kind of patience—meaning, that kind of confidence—all season. As recently as last month he seemed to flail at anything close to the strike zone.

Second chance, he springs out of that casual stance and slams a line single back through the box. Before you can say "Looking good," however, he's gunned down trying to steal second.

Third time up, he demonstrates his patience again by reaching another full count without taking a swing. Then, apparently looking for a fastball from the young, cornered pitcher, he looks bad when the confident right-hander puts a sharp breaking ball on the outside corner for strike three.

Leading off the bottom of the ninth with the Barons trailing 4–2, Michael yet again reaches a full count without swinging, then grounds out to third. The crowd starts draining out of the Met.

ROOKIE

A mere 1-for-4 for Michael, but a serious, competitive one. His confidence is up, but there's more. Those ol' mechanics the pros keep talking about—when Michael hits a line drive now, it's *hit*.

———

The Southern League weekly newsletter says that various big names have been following its clubs this week while the major leaguers sit: Bill Buckner with the Knoxville Smokies, Oakland manager Tony LaRussa with the Huntsville Stars, Cubs assistant GM Syd Thrift with the Orlando Cubs. During Chicks BP prior to Saturday's game, I walk down to the front row and introduce myself to Kansas City Royals manager Hal McRae, who's spending a few days looking at the Chicks.

Even at forty-nine, McRae looks as rock-solid as a Pro Bowl halfback, but like Buckner and many famous ballplayers I've seen, he's startlingly smaller up close than I had imagined. McRae is five-foot-ten or -eleven, and though solid, he's hardly a Hercules. But he banged out 2,091 hits and averaged .290 in nineteen big-league seasons, and though he was never a slugger, I can still picture "McRae, KC" year after year on the list of American League doubles leaders, back when I idly absorbed such things. Down the lines, into the gaps, off the walls, Hal McRae whacked the ball. Mechanics.

"I think Michael can make it," McRae says, "if he wants to put in the time. But I don't know how long he wants to give it. He needs another thousand at-bats in the minors. Two more years, maybe three. He's thirty-one now, so . . . "—and now, calculating, McRae looks doubtful—"two or three more years to get to the majors, then what? He plays a year or two and then he's going downhill physically." McRae knows that guys who play until they're forty-two, as he did, are rare.

Eureka!

"Anyway, he needs a thousand more at-bats in the minor leagues. And he's got to come back here next season, if he plays. Not necessarily for the whole season, but he needs to show he's mastered this league before he moves up to Triple A."

———

It's another pleasant evening at the Met, more of that end-of-a-shared-season feeling. The "special season" slant is all about Michael, but this communal feeling is about people like Nunie (Rogelio Nunez), the smiling Puerto Rican backup catcher who flattered me on my pitching last April. Nunie actually started hitting this season, when he got a chance to play (.295 overall, .317 in his last thirty-six games), but he's still a Double-A backup and his baseball future is uncertain. Yet in the break between warm-ups and gametime, while the Green View Lawn Care crew rakes and hoses and chalks, and the scoreboard operator puts up stumper questions for the fans, Nunie sits on the edge of the dugout roof signing autographs, smiling and talking with wide-eyed kids who see the twenty-four-year-old with the uncertain future as a grown, mature, secure *man*, a bigtime ballplayer.

The sight of Nunie brings to mind the two pitchers who threw to him at American Sports Medicine Institute back in April, with those little balls attached to their bodies, for White Sox conditioning expert Vern Gambetta and the ASMI cameras. Chicago native Al Levine, who started the season fast and whose wife had gotten a job at the mall, moved up to Triple A at Nashville in July, where he's gotten hammered. Mike Heathcott, coming back from shoulder surgery, got shelled in Birmingham and was sent down to the Single-A team, the Prince William Cannons, at Woodbridge, Virginia, where his fortunes improved only slightly. Next year, who knows?

ROOKIE

A few other Barons catch the communal end-of-season spirit and stand at the railing signing autographs. The little kids can't believe it. There's a cluster around the diminutive, low-key pitching coach, Kirk Champion. He's only a coach, not even an ex–big-leaguer coach—the Barons uniform is all that matters. Chris Pika would cause a stir by suiting up.

Michael, as per habit, stays in the clubhouse until last. When he does come out, as per habit, he doesn't sign. If he starts, there'll be no end to it.

Last thing before the game, a local drugstore sponsors Baby Races. A sheet of canvas about ten feet square, with painted stripes creating five lanes, is spread on the grass in front of home plate. With one parent at each end of each lane—one nudging the infant, "Go! Go!"; the other urging, "Come on! Come here!"—five infants are supposed to crawl the distance, winner take all. The babies don't know what's going on; they crawl a few inches, turn around, stray off, or simply sit staring at each other, while the grown-ups coax and beseech and the crowd laughs. Much later, it seems, one baby makes it from one end of the canvas to the other (though not quite in his lane) and wins a $20 gift certificate from the drugstore.

People keep streaming in through the early innings. Even the grassy standing-room areas beyond the bleachers down the left- and right-field lines are filling up. Hardekopf and Buccieri and Pika and the rest are buzzing around the park problem-solving, jabbering over their walkie-talkies about parking and hot dogs and the fourth-inning promotion, everyone pitching in. The show goes on.

Michael begins by looping a cheap single over the first baseman's head. Next he drills a sharp ground ball at the shortstop—an easy out, but good wood. They say the breaks

Eureka!

even out in baseball. In the bottom of the seventh he gets his due by smoking a clean single to center.

The crowd is announced as a remarkable 16,247— destroying the record of 13,751 set the night of Michael's first dinger a month ago and putting the Barons over their all-time single-season mark. It's a big night.

Michael whiffs in the ninth, but hey, everybody whiffs once in a while. Michael's strikeout rate is way down. Michael looks good.

Just in time.

Dave Campbell Believes

"The louder he talked of his honor, the faster we counted our spoons."

— Ralph Waldo Emerson

I wrap up the season with the Barons in Chattanooga.

It's been a showery day, and two hours before game time it's gloomy at Historic Engel Field: clouds hanging low, the smell of a storm in the air, the infield covered. I'm one of the few people in the park, sitting in the covered part of the bleachers and wondering if they're going to take off the tarp for BP and risk the skies opening up.

Presently I notice Mike Barnett out in front of the Barons' third-base dugout talking to a fiftyish man I don't recognize, who's also wearing a Barons uniform. When the conversation seems to be petering out, I walk down, let myself in through the gate by the dugout and sort of stand by, pad in hand, hoping for a few thoughts from Mike. He's got to be pleased with Michael's transformation, which also is the fruit of his own labors as batting coach. Take a bow, Mike.

"Mike?" He seems to be finished with the other man, and hearing his name called in an amiable tone, he turns my way with his typically amiable look—which, however, dissolves to one of horror in the split second it takes him to realize it's me.

"Mike? Can we talk a minute?"

Dave Campbell Believes

"Uhhh," Mike stammers, literally backing up, "I'd rather not, not right now . . . "

Not Mike, too. "No? Why not?"

"I'd just rather not," he says, with an effort at a smile. He doesn't want to be rude but he doesn't want to get too close, either. Whatever he's been told I'm carrying is *bad*.

"Isn't this kind of silly, Mike? You talk to everyone else. You've talked to me before."

"I'd just rather not," he repeats with the nervous smile. "If it's through our PR guys, OK, but otherwise I'd rather not."

"Under orders?"

"No, not under orders—I'd just rather not," Mike repeats, sounding curiously like Terry Francona a few weeks back.

"Just following the party line, huh?"

This time he doesn't even bother denying it. "Yeah, pretty much."

If Bill Hardekopf hadn't told me different, I'd swear it was a conspiracy.

———

When the tarp is at last rolled up and batting practice gets under way, I wind up chatting behind the cage with former big-league catcher Buck Martinez, now a TV analyst, who's doing tomorrow night's Barons-Lookouts broadcast for ESPN. A friendly guy—another *diminutive* guy, who lasted seventeen years in the majors!

Sunday was the first time he'd seen Michael, but Martinez is convinced he can crack the majors if he's willing to invest the time. "I believed it when I talked to him and saw his conviction, his commitment. I called my old teammate Garth Iorg up in Knoxville. We both played with Danny Ainge up in Toronto, and there are similarities, of course. I think Danny would have been a hell of a major-league player if he'd stayed with it.

"Garth said that early in the season you could see Michael's bat moving through the hitting zone, but the last time he saw him he had some quickness and some good swings. Garth actually said, 'If this guy had been playing since he was eighteen, there's no doubt in my mind he'd be an All-Star.' A pretty strong statement—Garth's seen a lot of ballplayers.

"From what I saw and heard, Michael was a robot early on, obsessed with mechanics, but now he's simplifying things. You have to. The best theory of hitting is still Rocky Bridges's theory: 'See ball, swing bat, hit ball, run like hell.' "

Eventually Martinez, with his pen and yellow legal pad, moves off to snag Lookouts manager Pat Kelly for an interview. When he returns, Martinez schmoozes with Barnett, whom I imagine he's never met; they're comfortable in ball talk, cracking each other up with Lou Pinella stories. Baseball men, dropping baseball names.

Michael, when he comes in to hit, hoots and joshes with his teammates. They make little beer bets on who can hit the most dingers as Michael, center fielder Kerry Valrie, and right fielder Kevin Coughlin take three rounds each in the cage, five or six cuts at a time. "Six-pack!" "Case if you don't hit *this* one out!"

"*Dôm Perignon*," Michael yells at Valrie, "if *you* hit one out!"

When Valrie teases him by refusing to hand over the weight that goes on the end of the bat for warm-up swings, Michael fakes a poke at Valrie's crotch with his black bat.

Most of the Lookouts, with BP over, are back in the clubhouse, but a half dozen are up in the first-base stands watching the Barons hit—watching Michael. A couple holler at him, causing Michael to look up, grinning: "Shee-it." And they holler some more.

Dave Campbell Believes

You get the impression Michael's having a good time now. It's not a frenzy at every stop anymore, and now he's got the fun and satisfaction of playing well and seeing his labors rewarded. You sense he'd like the season to be starting now instead of ending.

He's in a hurry to get better, and though he's made tremendous strides, he's constantly reminded how far he's got to go. Tonight he makes an outstanding catch racing to the left-field line but shows his mediocre arm on a long, looping throw to the plate. He looks bad at bat, flailing sadly at breaking balls he still doesn't seem to recognize until too late.

———

It's rainy again on Wednesday, and when they cancel batting practice and announce the game will be delayed, I head back up to Signal Mountain. ESPN's at Historic Engel Stadium, and if the game is played I can watch it from Chuck and Sarah's rec room.

The teams take the field after all, and Michael's evening is another mixed bag. After twenty-eight errorless games in the outfield, he muffs a ground ball in left, then bungles a long fly but is spared a second E by a generous official scorer. At bat, weak stuff . . .

My favorite moment comes when Dave Campbell, announcing the game with Buck Martinez, clarifies the origins of the Barons' bus for the national TV audience. They've been going on throughout about what a JesusChristamazing guy Michael is, so easy to talk to, so normal, so enthusiastic, on and on . . . *And not only that, he bought the team a bus!*

Five months after Michael did *not* buy the Barons a new luxury bus, five months after he invested not a single dime in the Barons' new accomodations, Dave Campbell not only tells America that he did—Dave's got the dialogue to prove it.

ROOKIE

"Michael said, 'I have the ability to do that, and I want to make my teammates comfortable.'"

What a guy.

Except there's not a mote of truth in it.

With the game tied in the eighth inning, the Barons score to go up 3–2. Michael comes up with the bases loaded. The Lookouts bring in right-handed reliever Scott Sullivan, but Michael, unfazed, gives the Barons some breathing room by looping a two-run single to right.

A clutch hitter, by the end of his first season.

———

No denying, the season ends on an up note. Michael's quiet in Huntsville the last weekend to wind up at .202—nothing to write home about, but he did bat .300 over the last couple of weeks and actually looked like a ballplayer.

Considering he was whacking the ball at the end, his season stats mean next to nothing, but for the record Michael played in 127 games and totaled 17 doubles (seventh among Barons), 1 triple, 3 homers, and 51 RBI (fourth). He drew 51 walks (third) and struck out 114 times (the most, by far). His strikeouts declined steadily each month until August, but that late-season rise came when he had stopped waving at every reachable pitch simply to avoid striking out and started working the count like real hitters do, trying to get a pitch he could *attack*. He was in trouble if he worked himself down to a last strike and then got one of those breaking balls he still wasn't recognizing in time, but the benefits to his maturing approach were borne out not only by the .300 mini-streak but by the sizzle on those late-season hits.

Michael tied for fifth in the Southern League with 30 stolen bases but got caught stealing 18 times. (Barons second baseman Doug Brady stole 34 and got caught 12 times.)

Dave Campbell Believes

He made 11 errors in the outfield, high among Southern League outfielders, and was moved from right field to left as a concession to his so-so throwing arm. On the other hand, he covered a lot of territory. Baseball men say he's an adequate defensive outfielder right now.

Meaning, he can make it if he can hit major-league pitching.

———

Michael was boffo box-office for the Southern League, which smashed its all-time single-season attendance record set last season. Several clubs established single-season records, largely due to the Barons, the most popular 65–74 team in the history of minor-league baseball. (The Barons finished in the middle of the pack for each official half of the Double-A season: 31–38 and 34–36.)

The Barons drew 467,867 at home—a new club record and the sixth-largest Double-A total in history. (The top five draws were the Nashville Sounds, from 1979 to 1983, before the club's move up to the Triple-A American Association.) The average crowd this season was 6,983—a major coup for a minor-league team. They're smiling at Suntory International.

Of course, it's not really a staggering number of people. It's not Elvis. There are a lot of people in Greenville and Memphis and Chattanooga, not to mention Birmingham, so crowds of 7,000 at home and 8,000 on the road indicate that a lot of people had better things to do. There's always a crush around Michael—that's why he and Mister Falk get lulled into thinking everyone on the planet is enthralled—but millions of bright people aren't in the crush, don't go to ballgames, couldn't care less about sports or athletes. They don't know anything about Michael Jordan except that he was a famous basketball player, and, knowing that, merely lump

ROOKIE

him with all pro basketball players as guys who happened to be freakishly tall and freakishly good at a high-paying game.

———

But Michael is surrounded by people who do care. In Huntsville, on the last stop of the season, he autographs the Jordancruiser on the door and under the driver's window, and the driver has the two spots clear-coated at a local body shop.

Not the City Council's Idea of a Hero

"When I speak of the importance to me of my reputation,
I am referring to a reputation that is deserved, not an
image cultivated for the public in spite of the facts."

— Arthur Ashe, *Days of Grace*

A few days after the end of the season, I see a short wire-service item in the *Atlanta Constitution* about an uproar in Birmingham over the Barons' notion of naming an inner-city ballfield after Michael's father, in honor of Michael. A couple of days later, I catch an item saying the Barons, under pressure, have withdrawn their proposal.

That's it. It's not as good a story as Michael buying a bus for the team. When I get back to Portland in late September, no one has heard about it at all.

Bill Hardekopf, who does return my phone calls now, tells me, "Michael had done so much for us that we wanted to make a permanent tribute to him. We sat around thinking of how we could do something nice and classy for the community and for Michael."

They decided it would be nice to name something after Michael's late father. They could donate a little money and send their grounds crew over to spruce up a field, which would become James Jordan Field.

ROOKIE

Bill says the Barons first called the Parks and Recreation Department in Hoover, the white bedroom community fifteen miles south of Birmingham that's been the Barons' home since 1988. It's also where Michael's Greystone residence and the Greystone Country Club are located. Bill says, "It was jointly decided that the money could be better spent in the inner city."

He next called the Birmingham Parks and Recreation Board. "They loved the idea and suggested the baseball field at Marconi Park." Marconi Park is located in Metropolitan Garden, the largest public housing project in Alabama. Little Leagues and softball leagues play there; bands practice there. "We ran it by several politicians—they loved the idea. We presented it to Michael, who was gone by then—we told him we wanted to do this as a tribute to his father, who provided so much inspiration to him, and to Michael for providing so much inspiration for kids to get turned on to baseball.

"The intent was never to cause an uproar. We saw it as kind of a win-win situation: we'd get this inner-city field fixed up, and Birmingham would have this tie with Jordan."

It was seen as a win-win situation for the Barons only: they'd be immortalized in the inner city, by way of Michael, in exchange for raking and chalking a Little League field and paying to have the grass cut a couple of times.

"We were just trying to do something nice," Bill Hardekopf says. "But flak developed from a couple of . . . I guess you'd call 'em *activists*, who said they had made requests for Michael to appear at functions that were important to them earlier in the season. Their requests went to Michael's agent in Washington, D.C., and they were apparently told that Michael couldn't make it to their events. So these guys were irritated and said that Michael didn't do anything for the inner city, so why should a field be named for his father there?"

Not the City Council's Idea of a Hero

But it wasn't only "a couple of activists" who found it odd that Hardekopf, a transplanted Californian representing a Japanese conglomerate, should propose naming something in Birmingham after Michael Jordan's *father*, who had no known ties to the city, in tribute to *Michael*, who had scarcely been seen inside the city limits except at after-dark spots like Sammy Go-Go's.

There's a little history here. According to Leon Evans, administrative assistant to city councilman William Bell, many people feel Birmingham has been disowned by the Barons. In the mid-1980s, the team's previous owner told the city that legendary Rickwood Field was outdated and he needed a new park. When the city agreed, the club made more demands. It was clear the Barons wanted out of Birmingham. Hoover, fifteen miles south, built Hoover Metropolitan Stadium and the Barons, forsaking the memories of Satchel Paige and Willie Mays, relocated in 1988.

"Birmingham feels snubbed by the Barons," Leon Evans says. "People wonder why, when Michael Jordan was assigned here and all these free tickets were given out to the Jefferson County Board of Education for the suburban kids, they weren't given to the Birmingham Board for the inner-city kids. OK, we accept that, but *then* when you come in and say you want us to name this field after Michael Jordan's father, in light of the fact that you didn't think of us when you were giving out those tickets . . . where's the benefit for us?"

Newstell Dowdell III, assistant to councilman Roosevelt Bell, says, "It was the mentality that 'We know what's best for you.' But the days of that kind of mentality are over. The feeling in Birmingham was, since Michael Jordan played in Hoover, and Hoover got all the money, why not name something *there* after him or his father?"

ROOKIE

The feeling was, why name anything at all after either of them? When Birmingham councilman Roosevelt Bell had requested Michael's appearance at the "Function in the Junction," an annual day of jazz and activities at economically depressed "Tuxedo Junction," he received a polite message from FAME saying Michael's schedule wouldn't permit it. "It was kind of funny," Dowdell recalls. "Along with the rejection they sent a Barons schedule and a poster of Michael. We thought, 'Thanks a lot.' "

Michael also couldn't make it to the Camp Birmingham Olympics, an annual competition for disadvantaged kids. He couldn't do anything for the local chapter of the Southern Christian Leadership Council. He was too busy for the development director at Miles College, a local black school.

He couldn't help Frank Matthews, "God's Gangster," a reformed gang member who heads the Youth Gang Alternative. Matthews called the Barons in August, after three gang-related killings in a week, trying to arrange to interview Michael on his "In Your Face" radio program.

All summer, administrators at Children's Hospital wondered why Michael never dropped in like other celebrities, many of whom are only passing through town.

Imagine my surprise at hearing Michael was too busy to help out. By all accounts he got in plenty of golf over the summer, and filmed juice and underwear and hot-dog commercials. I know from the authorized book *Michael Jordan: A Shooting Star* that Michael feels strongly about giving: "I want to help everybody but I can't. It's just a matter of us concerned people doing what we can through good thoughts, good prayers, and good deeds because we can make a difference."

Did Michael do *anything* in Birmingham?

"He came to the Birmingham Museum of Art," Leon Evans

says sarcastically, "to film a *Ball . . . Park . . . Franks* commercial.

"He wouldn't have had to do much to be appreciated," Evans goes on. "If he had come into the neighborhood for ten minutes and said, 'I'm glad to be in Birmingham,' whatever, I don't think the local officials would have had any opposition to accepting a donation from the Barons and naming the field. The people of Birmingham would have known Michael Jordan had come to Birmingham because they would have seen it on television. Now, I know he said he didn't come here to do bar mitzvahs and sign autographs, but he did do some of that, and it was always in the suburbs, never in Birmingham.

"Hardekopf told everyone that Jordan did something for the city when he played in a fundraiser at Birmingham Country Club. But people said, 'I can't even go to Birmingham Country Club!' And I don't know if the city fathers would say it this way, but to me, that is a place where blacks don't feel comfortable even if they can get in. The perception by blacks was that Birmingham Country Club isn't the inner city."

The press covers Birmingham Parks and Recreation Board meetings, and the Barons' pitch became public as soon as it was broached by the board.

All hell broke loose. People and organizations that FAME had rejected started coming out of the woodwork. Talk-radio lines were full of accusations and name-calling.

Before the parks board could bring the proposal to the city council for a vote, William Bell addressed the council requesting a resolution to reject the naming of anything after James Jordan, who had no connection with Birmingham, when there were so many worthy natives—the late John "Loch" Jordan, to name just one, an admired public servant who had become the highest-ranking black official in Alabama's Boy Scouts program.

Under fire, the Barons said they were sorry the whole thing had become so politicized and they were withdrawing their request to have the ballfield at Marconi Park named for Mr. Jordan. As a goodwill gesture, however, they were going to go ahead with their donation toward refurbishing the field.

The parks board received a check for $1,000 from the Barons—which, to keep things straight, was placed in the general fund instead of being earmarked for the field at Marconi Park.

It was a moot point once William Bell found out the amount of the Barons' donation. He called it an insult, asked the parks board to return the money, then walked around the Marconi Park neighborhood with a bucket and collected $1,700 in three hours.

That was pretty much the end of it. And in the end, the people who wanted Michael all summer don't know whether to blame Michael or the middlemen. "There's no way of knowing," says Newstell Dowdell III, "because you can't get to him. The Barons say all requests go to the agent in Washington, D.C. I don't know what happens then. I don't know if Michael even sees requests like ours. Maybe what you see on TV is just PR, but I think he's a guy who would have done at least a few appearances if we could have talked to him directly."

Who knows? I *did* talk to him directly, and thought I'd gotten his blessing, but Mister Falk had the last word.

———

With that chronic and uniquely American weakness for the supreme athlete, people have largely bought into Michael-the-media-creation, overlooking the dubious friendships and

Not the City Council's Idea of a Hero

his teammates' complaints and the blatant acquisitiveness. People wanted to believe he was as beautiful a guy as he was a basketball player. They got infinite help from the ads, because in the ads, he *was*.

Frank Rich, writing about O. J. in the *New York Times*, said, "In a country where there is no royalty and where, post-Watergate, politicians are held in almost universal contempt ... we want to believe in celebrities for the same reason we want to believe in God: their omnipotence and invulnerability, however illusory, hold out the promise that we, too, have a crack at immortality ... [O. J.'s] image, pristine only yesterday, was a fraud ... But that image couldn't have been sustained for so long without our will to believe in it."

Maybe we do have a need to look up to people. But we're realistic enough to know that most people aren't much better or worse than we are in any significant way (basketball talent doesn't qualify). We've found out too many times, in too many ugly ways, that even idols (*especially* idols) have feet of clay.

It's when someone is projected as better than "normal people," and then we find out it's a lie, that we object.

We wouldn't expect Michael or any player to spend $350,000 to buy his team a luxury bus. It's when he and his people let the world believe he did, and then we find out it's not so, that we object.

We just want people to be real. Michael and FAME and the money-men take such pains to make him *loved* with this crafted image of physical and moral perfection, sunny personality, preternatural innocence—and the irony is that the people who are ultimately loved are the ones who were simply real, who won us over precisely by being themselves and not giving two hoots. Muhammad Ali. John Lennon. Besides being beautiful and talented and bright and charming, they could be self-centered and self-serving; their growing pains could be embarrassing. In short, they were like us. We loved them because they were willing to admit it, and let it show, and not worry too much about what people thought.

Of course, they didn't have Michael's consideration of $31 million a year in endorsement contracts, which are based on the image of a man whose spiritual qualities are as extraordinary as his basketball skills—even if he has admittedly sold out, given up most of his freedom, and given his family short shrift.

Michael *has* to worry about what people think. But like a politician, he's worried about what people think of the *image*. If he cared about what we thought of him personally, he'd quit being a shill and be himself instead.

Whoever that is. I wonder if Michael has a clue anymore. Not long after I'm informed about the flap in Birmingham, I see that he released a statement through the Barons: "I was very surprised and happy with the Barons' suggestion to name a field after my father, but if the Birmingham community feels it would be more appropriate to name it after someone who better represents the city, then I certainly agree. It is unfortunate that some members of the community who questioned this donation did not go through the proper channels with regard to my personal schedule."

It's hard to think of the son of up-from-nothing James Jordan big-dogging people about going through proper channels—especially when they did go through channels, and have the letterhead rejections from FAME to prove it. I wonder if, God forbid, with his father gone Mister Falk's reptilian influence has become even greater.

Yet Michael's statement rated just a few lines in *Baseball Weekly*. No one back in Portland seems to have heard a word about the Marconi Park flap *yet*, meaning they never will. But

Not the City Council's Idea of a Hero

they all ask me, "Did you get a ride in that bus Jordan bought the team? Three hundred'n fifty thousand bucks, right?"

———

Michael's life is out of control. And how could he downsize his life now, even if he wanted to? He's as big as they get, which has brought him zillions of dollars—which is good, because he feels the need to build a twelve-foot wall around his 29,000-square-foot palace and buy pistols for protection and have $300,000 worth of high-tech security equipment installed at his son Jeffrey's school.

In order to fulfill his commitments to all these companies, he's away from his family almost all the time he's not playing ball.

When he is playing ball—traveling half the time, gone most of the time even when the team is at home, preoccupied all the time—there's not much point in having his family with him. Michael's wife Juanita and their three children never did move to Birmingham this summer, as originally (reportedly) planned.

Maybe it's too late to go back; Michael's existence, too distorted. He's surrounded by hustlers like Mister Falk who, while worrying about whether someone calls him an agent or a lawyer, earns his estimated $4.8 million per year (off Michael alone) by blithely telling councilmen and others that Michael doesn't have time, doesn't have time. He lives in a commercial world, constantly reassured that he's right and normal in wanting to amass as much wealth as possible, whatever the cost in personal terms. He's surrounded by people who admittedly owe their livelihood or their piddling sense of power to him and so do everything to keep getting results for him: make bucks, and keep Michael as clean as possible doing it.

ROOKIE

And where's it going? What's the goal? *More?*

In *Days of Grace*, Arthur Ashe wrote that even though he had won Wimbledon near the end of his career, he remained frustrated, still looking for a "culminating event" in his life. "My culminating event could never be physical, never something athletic. My culminating event had to be less personal and materialistic, more humanitarian and inclusive."

Well, Michael is young yet. He's imperfect like all of us, but he comes from a solid background and he's got a core of decency, even if it's getting lost in his mad existence. He could yet see the light and put his money and power and energy and charisma to work for something more significant—more humanitarian and inclusive—than his and Mister Falk's portfolios.

But it's hard to put toothpaste back in the tube. I wonder if he even remembers that his own baseball hero, Roberto Clemente, died trying to fly supplies in to earthquake victims in Nicaragua.

———

He remains a fascinating athlete, which was always the fascinating thing about him—not his money, his fame, certainly nothing he ever said or did in civilian clothes.

On one of the Barons' ESPN games, San Diego Padres batting champion Tony Gwynn said, "Teams don't have the time and money to invest in guys who are thirty-one years old and hittin' a buck-ninety [.190]. But because he's Michael Jordan he's gonna get that opportunity. A lot of people might think it's unfair to a lot of minor leaguers who've worked so hard to get there, but when the greatest athlete in the world says, 'I wanna play baseball for you,' you say, 'Well, suit up, Michael! Let's see what you can do!' "

The White Sox did, and so far they haven't been proven wrong. All things considered, Michael accomplished more than anyone could have reasonably expected, and he improved by leaps and bounds. Everyone remarked on his athletic ability and work ethic—which, together, put no limit on how much he could improve. He's got a long way to go to reach the major leagues, but by season's end I couldn't find a baseball man who would rule out the possibility.

Sports Illustrated's Steve Wulf, who wrote the cover story in the "Bag It, Michael!" issue back in April, told me, "I didn't think he had a chance to make it when I saw him in spring training. He had a terrible swing and just looked uncomfortable on the baseball field. But when I saw him in August, he looked like a baseball player. He had a terrific swing and he was hitting the ball on the screws. I'm a skeptic who's been convinced."

After playing in Scottie Pippen's charity basketball game (after all!) a few days after the Barons' season ended and scoring fifty-two points to remind us what we've been missing, Michael went to the Florida Instructional League for three weeks of work. According to Vern Gambetta, he had a great time with the young prospects and worked as hard as ever. Then it was on to the Arizona Fall League, a new operation comprising the six top prospects from each major-league organization—plus Michael, who was admitted at the special request of the White Sox. After a smash beginning Michael tailed off some, but overall his progress continued and there was talk he'd already been promoted to Nashville for the 1995 season. Sox GM Ron Schueler said he wasn't giving away the job in November, not on the basis of what Michael had accomplished in Birmingham—"but at his age, we can't have a three- or four-year plan."

ROOKIE

They're not ruling out the possibility that Michael can one day make the majors, and they want to find out. Not because he'll become the guy to bat behind Frank Thomas and lead the White Sox to the World Series, but because it's fascinating to see what a guy with optimal athletic ability, optimal determination, and optimal opportunity can accomplish in the skill-specific game of baseball in a short time. There's never been an experiment quite like it. It's what intrigued me in the beginning.

I'll keep watching. I say Michael makes it to the major leagues one day, and not just as a novelty when rosters are expanded at the end of the season. As a real major leaguer.

Imagine how big he'll be then.

———

Then again, how does he get any bigger? Mister Falk has been grabbing every opportunity for years.

On the glossy back cover of the October *Bus Ride* magazine, in a full-page color ad for Motor Coach Industry bus manufacturers, there's Michael, reclining oh-so-comfortably in a seat aboard the world-renowned Jordancruiser—the $350,000 luxury bus he didn't spend a dime on.